PRAISE FOR SAGE ROUNTREE

"Sage's clear approach to incorporating yoga into a training season perfectly addresses all the things athletes need to hear about flexibility and balanced conditioning—and Sage delivers it in a way that athletes can relate to."

—Karen Dubs, creator of the Flexible Warrior Athletic Yoga DVD series

"Yoga is not only *good* for athletes—it is essential, for both the physical and mental benefits. ... Sage shares the benefits that yoga has brought to her life as an athlete and offers easy-to-follow yoga postures and breathing techniques to help athletes of all sports get started with a safe and effective yoga routine and to help them avoid or rehabilitate an injury."

—Beryl Bender Birch, author of *Power Yoga* and *Beyond Power Yoga*, Director/Founder of The Hard & The Soft Yoga Institute, and contributor to *Yoga Journal*

PRAISE FOR *THE ATHLETE'S GUIDE TO YOGA*

"Endurance athletes generally have poor flexibility, core strength, balance, and posture. Improving these can really change performance for the better. *The Athlete's Guide to Yoga* is a great resource to get you on the path to better training and racing."

—Joe Friel, founder of Ultrafit and author of *The Triathlete's Training Bible*, *The Cyclist's Training Bible*, and *The Mountain Biker's Training Bible*

"*The Athlete's Guide to Yoga* is a practical in-your-body guidebook for anyone wanting to take their fitness routine into new realms. Clearly written, beautifully illustrated, it's a real resource for starting and deepening a practice that stays true to yoga's depth. Postures, breathing, relaxation, meditation, training routines, it's all here."

—Richard Faulds, Kripalu Center for Yoga & Health

"Somehow Sage Rountree has managed to maintain her yogic voice ... while also toning it down just enough to speak directly to an athlete. ... The book is straightforward without all the frou-frou and implied incense-burning and ohmmm of yoga that could turn off some athletes. ... Since she herself is a triathlete and runner, Rountree knows exactly where you get tight and why, what it feels like before and after certain workouts, the difficulties of combining a good yoga practice with hard training, and what's realistic or not for an athlete."

—SNEWS®

"Whether you're a yogini or you've never heard of downward-facing dog, you'll come away with something useful from *The Athlete's Guide to Yoga*."

—*Women's Adventure* magazine

"This comprehensive book on yoga for athletes makes a compelling case for why and, more importantly, how athletes of every stripe can benefit from making yoga a regular part of their workout regimens."

—American Council on Exercise Get Fit

PRAISE FOR *THE ATHLETE'S POCKET GUIDE TO YOGA*

"This sweet little book is a delightful and abundant source of yoga pose sequences. *The Athlete's Pocket Guide to Yoga* is a great resource for yoga teachers and an easy source of inspiration and guidance for beginner to intermediate yogis."

—YogaBasics.com

"For time-crunched yogis and jocks who don't even identify with the term yogi but want a good stretch or cross-training workout, take a look at *The Athlete's Pocket Guide to Yoga*. With no need to attend a class or even watch a DVD, there's no excuse to not get a few poses in."

—GearJunkie.com

the RUNNER'S
GUIDE TO YOGA

sage rountree

the RUNNER'S
GUIDE TO YOGA
A PRACTICAL APPROACH
TO BUILDING STRENGTH & FLEXIBILITY FOR BETTER RUNNING

Boulder, Colorado

3002 Sterling Circle, Suite 100
Boulder, Colorado 80301-2338 USA
(303) 440-0601 · Fax (303) 444-6788 · E-mail velopress@competitorgroup.com

Distributed in the United States and Canada by Ingram Publisher Services

Library of Congress
Cataloging-in-Publication Data
Rountree, Sage Hamilton.
The runner's guide to yoga: a practical approach to building strength and flexibility
for better running / Sage Rountree.
p. cm.
Includes bibliographical references and index.
ISBN 978-1-934030-84-4 (pbk.: alk. paper)
1. Hatha yoga. 2. Running—Training. I. Title.
RC1220.Y64R687 2012
613.7'046—dc23
2012000698

For information on purchasing VeloPress books,
please call (800) 811-4210 ext. 2138 or visit www.velopress.com.

Cover and interior design by Vicki Hopewell
Cover and interior photographs by Cindy Hamilton
Composition by Jane Raese

Text set in Bembo.

12   13   14 / 10   9   8   7   6   5   4   3   2   1

TO MOM

We must be still and still moving
Into another intensity
For a further union, a deeper communion.

—T. S. Eliot

CONTENTS

Preface   xi
Acknowledgments   xiii
Introduction   xv

PART I: OVERVIEW: HOW YOGA HELPS RUNNERS   1

  1 Strength and Flexibility   3
  2 Balance   9
  3 Focus   15

PART II: POSES FOR STRENGTH AND FLEXIBILITY   21

  4 Hips and Thighs   23
  5 Core   51
  6 Lower Legs   73
  7 Upper Body   81

PART III: FINDING THE RIGHT BALANCE   91

  8 Preventing and Correcting Overuse Injury   93
  9 Preventing Acute Injury   105
  10 Balancing Work and Rest   113
  11 Balancing Studio Yoga with Home Practice   117

PART IV: EXERCISES FOR FOCUS   127

  12 Yoga's Eight-Limbed Approach   129
  13 Breath Exercises   139
  14 Meditation Exercises   147

PART V: PUTTING IT TOGETHER   **155**

15 Routines for Dynamic Warm-up Before a Run   157
16 Routines for Practice During a Run   171
17 Routines Following an Easy Run   175
18 Routines Following a Hard Run or Race   185

Recommended Resources   199
Subject Index   205
Poses Index   213
About the Models   219
About the Author   221

PREFACE

Running and yoga go together like yang and yin. While at first they may seem disparate, they are instead complementary. And just as the Taoist yin-yang symbol displays a circle of the yang in the yin and a circle of the yin in the yang, running and yoga each hold space for the other at their core.

While running involves moving forward through space, covering miles of ground at a time, a yoga practice is usually confined to a 2.5-by-6-foot mat. But both involve using the mind, body, and breath in unison to test—and often to surpass—the boundaries of what we think we can do. While running involves doing, pushing, working, a yoga asana practice is often about being, yielding, resting. But both require and develop the athlete's intuition about when and how much to strive, when and how much to surrender. While running can emphasize numbers such as mathematical progressions of mileage and interval pace and team or series points, yoga eschews much scientific categorization. But both teach us to follow the voice within. And while running can seem to be about competition, yoga can seem to shun competition. But we learn from both that we create competition from our own minds and that it can push us to perform and grow in wonderful ways.

In my classes and in this book, I teach about intention, form, and breath. We need to be clear on our intention—our reason for doing the workout, our goal for the race, our resolve for the yoga practice. Once intention is clear, it helps us use the most efficient form for the task at hand and the right breath to support that form. When we run, proper form creates endurance by using only the energy we need. When we practice yoga poses, we need to engage the right muscles to support the shape and then relax everywhere else. In both, we need to use the breath that supports the demands on the body.

My intention for this book is to share tools that will help you find the right balance between running and yoga, between doing and being, and between moving through the world and investigating inner experience. This book is not a comprehensive treatise on the yoga system or even yoga poses, but instead covers the elements of yoga that work best for runners. And I want to use the breath—here, the voice—that supports the form, speaking in language grounded in the body but open to the more spiritual aspects of both running and yoga.

Thank you for reading.

ACKNOWLEDGMENTS

Yoga is a teacher-based system. While our experience of transformation happens through a diligent personal practice, the tradition is handed down from one teacher to another, and I owe a huge debt of gratitude to my own teachers. In particular, Michael Johnson and Leslie Kaminoff have expanded my understanding of the *Yoga Sutras* in wonderful ways that directly influenced Chapter 12, and Leslie's teachings on many subjects, especially the breath, inform much of my understanding of the yoga system. Thanks to them and to all my teachers, including Ruth Newnam, whose class I have especially enjoyed attending throughout the drafting of this book. Thanks also to my coach, Joan Nesbit Mabe, for her teachings and her own exploration of the ways yoga and running intersect. And thanks go to my assistant teachers and students who have been enthusiastic in their support of my work, especially Emilie Smith, Kristen Engles, Terry Cockburn, and Petra Ledkovsky.

The photo shoot for this book took place at my studio, the Carrboro Yoga Company. I'm grateful to my co-owner, Lies Sapp, for making it such a lovely, warm place, which comes through in the photos. My students Thomas Graham and Kristin Watson, both wonderful athletes, graciously modeled the ways these poses appear when assumed by real runners. Supporting behind the scenes, our teacher-trainees made wonderful assistants, and I send huge thanks to Alexandra DeSiato, Francesca Morfesis, Emily Padgett, Greg Smith, and Jennifer Weaver for helping the shoot go so smoothly. The wonderful team at prAna were incredibly generous—and fast—with sending clothing for the shoot. And it was a great chance to collaborate professionally with the gifted photographer Cindy Hamilton, whom I am proud to call Mom.

As ever, my publishing team have been wonderful, knowing when to push me and when to let me rest, like any good coach. Casey Blaine and Renee Jardine mapped out the season plan by sharpening the concept for the book; Connie Oehring and Beth Partin held me accountable workout to workout by making sure each sentence hit the mark. Bob Kern and Dave Trendler make wonderful cheerleaders from the start and finish line.

Special thanks go to the day-to-day support crew in my life: my students, my coaching clients, and my running group, the Janes. Your positivity and support make my work (and workouts) that much more wonderful. Thanks, finally, to those with whom I spend time in both stillness and motion: my husband, Wes, and our daughters, Lily and Vivian.

INTRODUCTION

In this book, we will investigate how yoga will help your running. You'll learn how yoga can prevent and correct running injuries, how yoga can make you feel (and yes, even look) better, and how yoga will give you new focus and tenacity with a direct positive effect on your running. We will explore which of the hundreds of yoga poses, exercises, and techniques to use, and I'll explain why, how, and when to use them. In this book, then, you'll find concrete advice on how to use yoga to be a better runner and a happier person.

Instead of being a comprehensive catalog of every pose—for a more thorough look at the poses, please read my book *The Athlete's Guide to Yoga*—this book covers poses of special use to runners, focusing on those that are safe for home practice. (Handstand, for example, can be a great teacher of proper alignment in both yoga and running, but it's best learned in the presence of an experienced yoga educator.) Here, I'll introduce yoga to those who are new to the practice and help those with some experience develop a home practice to complement their running.

In Part I, we'll look at how yoga helps runners by conferring strength, flexibility, balance, and focus in both physical and psychological ways. The second part of the book describes poses to use to improve running, targeting the main regions of the body we use in running: the hips and thighs; the core; the lower legs; and the upper body. In this section, we'll talk about why and how to do these poses and how you can modify them to make them more or less intense. In Part III, we explore ways to use yoga for balance. Being balanced in your body, in space, and in your approach to work and rest is critical for injury prevention. We'll move on to yoga philosophy in

Part IV, as we investigate the mental and spiritual aspects of the practice in ways that will hone your focus and sense of well-being. Finally, Part V details when to do these poses and exercises, outlining routines for practice before, after, and even during your runs and races.

Using the techniques outlined in this book, you'll learn more about yourself: where your perceived limits are and how to surpass them, when to push and when to back off, how to follow your breath and your intuition, and how to use competition to achieve peak performance.

PART I

OVERVIEW:
HOW YOGA
helps
RUNNERS

1

STRENGTH AND FLEXIBILITY

I HATED THE FIRST yoga class I attended. The problem wasn't my flexibility; while some of the stretches were intense, I was familiar enough with stretching and didn't have a problem twisting my body into the shapes the teacher described. The problem was that yoga was hard—much harder than I'd expected—in its demands on my strength. We were talked into a pose and then held it for what felt like minutes on end while the teacher worked the room, offering adjustments. *Oh, no,* I thought, *he's forgotten we're all in this pose! I've been abandoned! My muscles are burning; my legs are shaking—how is this generating inner peace?* I left with legs like jelly, feeling humbled and much, much weaker than I thought myself to be.

Perhaps your experience will be the opposite. You may find the strength poses doable while the flexibility poses flummox you. Each of us has individual strengths and weaknesses. Often we have a deficiency in either strength or flexibility; sometimes we are lacking in both. The rare individual—including yoga practitioners—will maintain a healthy, dynamic balance between the two, exhibiting strength and flexibility in equal measure.

What eventually brought me back to yoga was knowing that I needed balance in my body. I'd built strength in my marathon training, but I could feel my flexibility waning. By adding a 90-minute class once a week and revisiting a few poses at home after my runs, I brought my body back into enough balance to finish my first marathon in just under four hours. In addition to the hip strength and leg flexibility that kept me on pace through the race, yoga helped me cultivate mental strength and a flexible attitude that enabled me to weather the highs and lows that come over the course of 26.2 miles. Yoga can help you find that same balance between strength and flexibility, whether your goal race is 100 meters or 100 miles.

Sthira and *Sukha*

The *Yoga Sutras*, a centuries-old series of aphorisms that define yoga, explain the method for quieting the fluctuations of the mind so that the practitioner can connect to his or her true nature (see Chapter 12 for an exploration of the sutras). Over the course of almost 200 verses, little reference is made to the physical practice—what most of us in the twenty-first-century West think of as yoga. The sutras' take on the postures is *Sthira sukham asanam*. The Sanskrit translates, loosely, to this: The posture (*asana*) should be both firm (*sthira*) and easy (*sukha*).

These twin concepts, effort and ease, stability and mobility, strength and flexibility, must be present simultaneously. This concept applies not just to sitting in meditation (what the sutras are most likely prescribing) but to all physical activity, where we must balance a rigidity of form (in the skeleton, for example) with a fluidity of motion (in the muscles, for example). And it applies to running, too, where we must balance stiffness of form with a fluid range of motion.

STIFFNESS

Think of elite runners. What words would you use to describe their form? *Springy, snappy, floating.* This comes from *sthira*, stiffness. Good runners are tight in the right places. Stiffness around the hips and core is critical for efficient transfer of energy to the ground and for recoil that takes the energetic rebound from the ground and rolls it into forward motion. A runner who is too lax around the hips or weak around the core will sink into the ground with each step. This is inefficient running, and it can lead to injury over time, as the joints are strained by excessive torque.

Through running, you will develop sport-specific strength. There's a reason that runners are obsessed with mileage: Generally speaking, running more miles confers efficiency, building strength in the hips and core muscles that supports a more economical stride. That means less effort at the same pace or greater ability to run faster paces.

RANGE OF MOTION

If you have had, at times, trouble reaching your shoelaces, then you know there is certainly such a thing as too much stiffness. While you need strength to run well, you also need enough flexibility and ease (*sukha*) to move fluidly through the proper range of motion and to access your strength. Too much stiffness in your hips can shorten your stride, thus limiting your speed, which is a factor of your stride rate and your stride length. Tightness in a specific muscle can alter your stride, as you subconsciously develop a little hiccup to work around it, and such gait modification can cause a host of problems up and down the kinetic chain of your body: knee trouble, foot issues, back pain.

Developing appropriate flexibility in the muscles will allow you to find the most efficient patterns for your stride. Greater mobility in the joints of the feet, hips, and spine will ease strain in these areas and others, preventing injury and lending an overall sense of well-being.

WORK AND REST

We also see this balance between *sthira* and *sukha* in proper run training. Both hard workouts and easy recovery runs are necessary for the body to receive the proper dosage of stress and to take the time to adapt to the stress and grow stronger. The same holds true in your yoga practice. There will be times to work and times to rest.

I cover the balance between work and rest in more detail in Chapter 10, but for a much more detailed look at recovery and ways to support hard work with high-quality rest, please refer to my book *The Athlete's Guide to Recovery.*

How Yoga Builds Strength

As I discovered in my first yoga class, a physical yoga practice can quickly reveal the limitations of your strength. It can also work to build your strength, challenging your muscles in both isometric and isotonic exercises.

Isometric strength develops when you hold a pose for a long time, forcing your muscles to work against static resistance. This could mean pushing your feet into the floor in a warrior pose or holding your hands to the ground in plank. Maintaining the position in a static hold and working against the steady resistance of the floor is key here. Such long holds develop the strength that helps you hold your core steady while you run.

Isotonic strength, however, comes from dynamic motion in and out of poses, as the muscles contract concentrically (while shortening) and eccentrically (while lengthening) as you move rhythmically. Your arm and leg muscles work in the same way as you run. Building isotonic strength will support your running.

Yoga poses use your body strength for resistance, but they are not a direct replacement for a strength-training program using weights. For some runners, yoga can suffice as a strength practice; for others, a gym-based routine is useful. If you are an efficient runner and powerful on hills, yoga may be a strength practice. If you are weak compared to others in your training and age group, combine yoga with a gym-strength routine.

Many yoga classes feature a practice that moves forward and backward on the mat. Rectangular mats are set up with the short side forward, and the yogis move from front to back in sun salutations, standing poses, and even floor routines. For runners, this serves to build strength in the sagittal plane of forward motion—where we spend most of our time.

Yoga can also help build strength side to side. More and more yoga styles are bringing students out of this linear plane—one runners are stuck in almost exclusively, as endurance sports emphasize forward motion—and into sideways motion and spiraling twists. Look for rooms where the mats are laid out horizontally, or classes with "mandala" or "free flow" in the title. This approach is of great benefit to runners because it cultivates balance.

How Yoga Increases Flexibility

The flexibility you can gain through a physical yoga practice is extremely useful for your running. Proper stretching helps you balance the relationship between muscles in your body, loosening tight muscles that hamper a fluid, full range of motion.

In yoga's static stretches (poses held for a period of 30 seconds to two minutes or longer), you will stretch not only muscles but also, with longer holds, the fascia that surrounds and shoots through your muscles. This connective tissue can be elastic, but it can also stick to itself like a wad of plastic wrap. Proper stretching helps to smooth it back out.

Yoga also moves dynamically, in sequences in which practitioners go from pose to pose with the breath. Dynamic movement aids flexibility in the muscles and emphasizes smooth, healthy range of motion at the joints. Lack of mobility at the joints can strain ligaments, tendons, and muscles and reduces efficiency. Hypermobility at the joints can cause problems, too, but in most devoted runners, the trend is toward stiffness rather than the excessive range of motion exhibited by dancers and gymnasts. Your goal will be to build enough flexibility to run with a full range of motion.

Finding the Right Balance

Most runners carry an imbalance of some sort: top to bottom, side to side, work to rest. In Part III, we'll look at self-tests you can use to determine where your own imbalances lie. Many yoga poses naturally create balance by strengthening one part of the body and stretching another. A lunge, for example, strengthens the front leg while stretching the back leg. At the same time, a lunge requires balance between the inner and outer thighs, the front and back of the torso, and the upper and lower body. Some poses focus more on strength, others target flexibility, and still others balance strength and flexibility by focusing fully on rest.

Yoga will help you balance strength and flexibility by increasing both and teaching you which types of exercises will best balance your needs. By cultivating balance, you'll be able to run more mileage, faster, with less physical and mental effort. This balance is the focus of Chapter 2.

2

BALANCE

THE WORD yoga means "union," coming from the Sanskrit *yuj*, for "yoke," the wooden bar that can be placed on the necks of two oxen to direct them to work together. The practice connects two powerful forces that could go in opposite directions and harnesses them to work toward a single goal. These forces often appear to oppose each other: mind and body, stiffness and flexibility, running and lying on the floor breathing. But the practice of yoga connects these forces and works to strike a dynamic balance in the body so that we can turn our attention to connecting in other areas (emotionally, mentally, and spiritually). This balance serves you well as a runner, not least in helping to prevent injury.

Balance is the key to injury prevention, as all running injuries are the result of imbalance. Overuse injuries, the most common injuries runners endure, result from a muscular or structural imbalance. For example, if your hips are relatively weak, the iliotibial (IT) band may take up the stabilizing work that should be performed by the hip muscles. Or if your quadriceps are too tight relative to your hamstrings, they will exert too much force on your kneecap, making it track wrong and irritate the soft tissue around it. By maintaining balance in your body—front to back, side to side, top to bottom—you're actively preventing overuse injuries.

Imbalance also causes acute injuries. For example, out on the trail or road, you can literally lose your balance in space and fall, winding up with cuts, scrapes, or broken bones. In the case of a fall or a collision with another runner, the force that's coming at you is stronger than—and thus out of balance with—the force that your body applies to it. Chapter 9 will help you gauge your own sense of balance in space.

Finally, mental injuries such as burnout come from an imbalance between the amount of work you are doing and the amount of rest you are taking. Yoga will help you find balance in all these areas. We will explore this concept in detail in Part III.

Balance Within the Body

The physical yoga practice develops balance in the body. A well-rounded yoga practice that includes standing postures, backbends, forward folds, side bends, twists, and inversions will naturally increase your balance top to bottom, front to back, and side to side. This is why yoga classes work, especially at first. A class with a generic mix of poses will organically address the whole body, and the imbalances most of us accrue in our running and our lives diminish. You may come to class with a slight forward tilt to your pelvis caused by strong, short hip flexors, and the person on the mat next to you may have a backward tilt to the pelvis because of shorter, tighter hamstrings. Both of you, practicing wisely, will find more freedom—you through backbends and lunges, your neighbor through forward folds.

To find a more personal balance, begin a home practice that targets your specific needs. The poses and techniques outlined in this book will help. Your needs will shift over time, depending on your training, the amount of time you spend standing and sitting each day, and your age. Home practice, or private lessons with an experienced teacher, will give you the opportunity to evaluate your needs and work to keep the body in dynamic balance. *Dynamic* is key here: What works at one point in the training cycle isn't necessarily the right thing for another point. Pay attention to your body, breath, and mental experience, and you'll be able to adjust your yoga practice—and your training—to maintain a healthy balance.

Balancing the Body in Space

Yoga will improve your running by increasing your sense of just where your body is in space and how to move your body through space. The postures charge you to think about the placement of your hands, your feet, your pelvis, and your shoulders. By increasing your awareness of what your pelvis, spine, and limbs are doing, you forge neural connections between your brain and your muscles. This increases your ability to activate the smaller stabilizing muscles in your lower legs, improving your balance on the road and, importantly, on the trail.

Through yoga, you'll develop a stronger sense of where you are relative to the road or trail and to other runners. You'll know better how to stay light on your feet and when to push to cover a surge from the competition. Likewise, you'll grow aware of opportunities to attack. And if you should begin to lose your balance, you'll have a nimbler step and be able to recover quickly by realigning your center of gravity.

Balance in the Mind, Body, and Spirit

Yoga fosters connection: a balance between areas in the body, a balance of the body in space. It also connects the body with something more. You'll get more balanced in your mind-body connection through your yoga practice, growing more aware of the ways in which your mind and body relate. You'll discover and refine ways to keep your mind focused when your body is in an intense situation such as a race or hard run, and ways to use your mind to relax your body for maximum efficiency.

Yoga also balances this internal, intrapersonal connection of mind and body with an interpersonal connection of you to others. Through yoga, you'll increase your awareness of how we are all connected. One method is to breathe together in class. The breath quite literally connects each of us to the other as we sit together and breathe. For cross-country teammates, this connection is critical. Anyone who's ever been swept along by a crowd at a race or silently paced by a newfound friend on the trail recognizes this connection as palpable and powerful.

Balancing Work and Rest

Yoga balances your running by serving as the yin to its yang—and, at certain points in the season, the yang to the relative yin of your easy running periods. Yoga offers a chance to focus on being instead of doing, on remaining still instead of covering terrain while running. This balance plays out across the training cycle, at both the macro- and microlevels. Yoga's role is to complement your training at the level of the season, the month, the week, the day, and even the workout. Chapter 10 will help you test this.

SEASON

Your yoga practice may vary from season to season. When you begin yoga, you'll face a learning curve. After overcoming your initial confusion, you may find yourself getting quite enthusiastic about yoga, looking for stronger, harder, or more sophisticated classes, like the runner who gets the marathon bug and rushes to run a marathon in the first season or two of regular running. While the enthusiasm is admirable, the body may break down if the physical practice is more than the athlete can absorb. Better to slowly deepen and build your practice, keeping an eye on how it affects your training and the rest of your life. If you push too hard, too soon—in yoga or in running—you may find yourself either injured or burnt out on the discipline and wind up walking away from something that could be a hugely positive force in your life.

MONTH

Choose a yoga practice that will bring balance to your training month to month. Most runners follow a training plan that builds cyclically, starting with base mileage at an aerobic effort, moving into strength- and speed-focused blocks, and peaking with a race-simulation phase and then a race or series of races. Each block lasts three to four weeks, ideally with some scheduled downtime. During these step-back weeks, your body absorbs the hard work of the cycle; it's a good time to also scale back your yoga practice.

As you choose poses and classes, look to foster balance between running and yoga. An easy base period of running is a good time to take up or deepen a practice, with an emphasis on building strength through standing poses and possibly through harder studio classes. As the intensity of your run training increases, you'll need to assess the intensity of your yoga practice and ensure that you're not undermining your hard running work by pushing too hard on the mat. Choose poses that maintain core strength and hip flexibility, and allow plenty of time for rest and recovery.

When entering your peak period, pull back even further. In this cycle, you should enjoy a mellow physical yoga practice, sticking to gentle and restorative classes or using your home practice to help you recover. That doesn't mean you can't have a dedicated daily practice—it just shouldn't be too physically demanding. Instead, sharpen your mental focus with breathing exercises and meditation, as described in Part IV of this book.

WEEK

You'll also want to find the right balance of yoga and running over the course of your week. Again, the principle of inverse proportion applies. When you're doing a long or intense run, let your yoga practice be gentle and easy. When you're running easy, if you are months from competition, it's alright to push a little in a more physical practice. On medium-intensity run days, for example, those when you're doing a tempo effort, a medium-intensity practice focused on core and hips is in order.

One note about inverse proportion: Keep your rest day sacred. Don't go hard in your yoga practice just because you aren't running. Choose a very easy series of poses or rest entirely.

DAY

Part V of this book shows where yoga can fit in your day: before, during, and after runs. You'll best balance your body by considering the physical demands of your day and choosing a practice to fit it. If you sit in a car or at a desk for much of the day, finish your run with a few stretches for the legs and hips and then slot in some passive backbends to open the chest and front of the hips after your day of sitting.

WORKOUT

When you take the time to check in with your intention and to be clear on your goals for the workout, you'll balance the physical nature of your workout with a clear sense of mental purpose. You'll be able to best see how to direct your energy, when to push, and when to relax.

3

FOCUS

BEYOND ITS MANY physical benefits, yoga teaches you focus. Focus develops organically through the physical practice and breath exercises, and it is also the subject of the more esoteric limbs of yoga, as we will see in Chapter 12. Running teaches focus as well. You must constantly return your awareness to the present moment, evaluating your pacing, your perceived exertion, your position relative to the competition. If you are running trails, focus is critical to remaining upright on uneven ground. (Have you traced your falls to losing your focus, if only for an instant?) For the runner, yoga will present some very familiar situations. Deep in a pose, you'll find you're tempted to let your attention wander. Return to focus by bringing your awareness back to your body in the moment and developing the most efficient form you can, given the demands of what you're doing. Then come back to your breath, using the breath that's appropriate for the task at hand.

Snapping Back

In both yoga and running, you need to keep your focus on the task at hand. Otherwise, the smallest problem will get you off track. This is part of the process. Don't try to maintain an unbroken focus. Instead, simply return to what you are doing every time you lose focus. If you are particularly distracted, be grateful: You have extra opportunities to practice!

ON THE RUN

Notice what pushes you out of focus. If the problem is one you can control—an issue of pacing or nutrition—address it as best you can and then get back to the run.

ON THE MAT

If you fall out of tree pose in class, instead of standing there, waiting for the rest of class to finish, move back into it. If you fall out of tree pose at home, instead of moving on to the next pose, return to tree and hold it. Some days are wobbly days; some poses are always challenging; one side of your body may be less stable and more mobile than the other. Observe these patterns and return to the task at hand.

Endurance

The keys to endurance are efficient form and focus. It's that simple! As you train and as you practice yoga, constantly return to the most efficient form you can muster. In both, that usually means finding mountain pose: aligning your feet, knees, and hips; bringing your pelvis to neutral; engaging your transversus abdominis; keeping your spine long; relaxing your shoulders; dropping your chin slightly; and reaching up through the crown of your head. That's a lot to think about, but the more you practice returning to mountain pose alignment, the easier it becomes.

You'll also need to reinstate the appropriate breath for what you're doing. If you're doing a long run at an easy pace, your breath should flow naturally and allow you to carry on a conversation. If you're running a tempo effort, your breath is probably more rhythmic, tied to your footfalls. When you progress to a harder effort, your breath may move quite fast. But whatever your pace, you can usually find a way to relax and smooth your breath, even a tiny amount. Such reductions in effort and energy consumption allow you to maintain efficient form a little bit longer. That's endurance.

Form and breath entertain you when you're bored, giving you something to think about. And at the other end of the spectrum, when you are working very hard, paying attention to form and breath gives you a laser focus. Best of all, "form and breath" makes a lovely mantra of its own, suitable for repetition both as a mental focusing tool and as a cue to return to the most efficient alignment and breathing you can.

ON THE RUN

Running, by definition, involves effort. Sometimes it's a light effort; sometimes it's a hard one. But there will always be muscular and cardiovascular exertion, leading to a different bodily state than you'd have maintained sitting on the couch. Putting out effort can create a cascading effect: You're working hard in your legs, so you start to tense your arms more than you need to, and soon your fists ball up into white-knuckled knots. Or the breath adjusts to suit your new pace and then continues to speed up even though it doesn't need to.

When you find this happening, come back to the most efficient form and breath you can. Notice where the effort exists in your body and question whether it's necessary. You can do this through a full-body scan. Start at your feet. Notice where they hit the ground. Could your footstrike be cleaner? Next, move to your lower legs. Are they kicking out to the sides behind you, or swinging sideways as you lift your knees? Relax in these areas if you can. Notice the sensation in your quadriceps, hamstrings, and glutes. Is one muscle group talking to you louder than the others? Can you relax a little so they work in harmony? What is the angle of your pelvis? Would dropping your tailbone toward your heels and pulling your belly in slightly help you relax more?

Give the same attention to the upper body. Could your arms swing more smoothly? Are they tracking straight to the midline, not across it? When you pull your elbows back, are you opening or closing the bend at your elbow? Could you get by with less? What's going on with your hands—could you relax them a little more and conserve energy? Your shoulders may be tensing; release tension there and let your shoulder blades slide toward the back of your waistline. Keep your chest open so that your breath can move freely; closing your chest off by hunching your back or holding your arms too high inhibits the free flow of the breath.

Finally, feel your neck and head. Is your chin jutting forward? Would relaxing more allow you to drop it down, relieving tension in the back of your neck?

When you've finished the body scan, turn your attention to your breath, giving it the same inquiry: Is this the right way to breathe now? Compare what you find with what you have seen in previous training sessions and adjust as needed. Look for a free, uninhibited breath during easy efforts and a smooth, rhythmic breath during hard efforts. See Chapter 16 for more on breath exercises to practice while running.

ON THE MAT

Make a similar investigation when you are on the mat. Some poses, such as standing poses, will certainly require effort to maintain, just as running does. And just as in running, you're likely using more energy than you need to while practicing them. Scan your body and see where you can relax more while holding the pose. In single-legged standing balance poses, it may be that your standing foot is doing more work than it should; relaxing it can make the pose steadier. In other standing poses, you may be holding too much effort in your muscles and cutting off the free flow of energy that would help you maintain the pose longer.

Other poses need no muscular tension at all; they are best served when you fully relax. If you're finding that hard to do, ask yourself whether you've overreached with the setup of the pose. You may have set it up too intensely, leading to an unconscious pushing to lift yourself out of the pose. (This is easy to feel in pigeon forward fold, for example.) Then do your full-body scan.

It's common in deep hip openers to focus very hard on relaxing the muscles around the hips but then to accrue tension in another area of the body. Often, it's the shoulders, neck, and jaw. Our goal in relaxing poses is to clear out tension entirely, not to smear it from one area of the body to another. To help dissolve tension, use your breath. Take deep breaths, inhaling into the areas where you feel tension and exhaling to release it. Your breath serves to release the toxins you are done with. Let it also be the porter for tension you'd like to remove from your muscles.

Conferring Perspective

Your running and your yoga should both have a purpose. Think about why you run. These reasons probably have to do with health, fitness, self-knowledge, self-improvement, the ability to push and reach the goals you've set for yourself. Get very clear on the big picture of why you are running. Once this overarching intention is set, you'll be able to create subgoals and to keep perspective when things get tough.

ON THE RUN

Consider your goals for the season. Are you tackling a new race distance? Are you aiming to set a personal record? To qualify for the Boston Marathon? Once you are clear on the season's goals, you can make decisions in service to those goals. This applies to everything from which workouts to do to what paces to run to what terrain you run on. It also applies to what to wear, what to eat, and when to rest.

At the start of each workout, take a moment to consider the goals of that workout. Is the intention to run long and slow, to build your endurance and aerobic system? To run a tempo pace, working on lactate clearance? To sharpen your upper-end speed and increase your maximum oxygen uptake? When you are clear on this intention, it will be easier to maintain the right form and the fullest breaths that serve it during your workouts.

ON THE MAT

Use the same process on your mat. Take a moment to consider the goals of this session. Are you seeking to use restorative poses and breath exercises to relax after a long day? To increase your flexibility with deep stretches? To build strength and balance in standing postures? Or is your intention less physical: to be present with whatever emotions arise, to let go of self-criticism, or to feel your breath moving in and out, using that as a link to the moment?

When you are clear on the reasons you're practicing, you'll be able to make choices that align with this intention. That can mean doing poses that suit your goals at home or adjusting yoga practice in class by resting when needed or by using the energy of the group to help you challenge yourself. When you get distracted or when things get intense, refocus on your intention, realign your choices with your resolve, and use the energy you need in service to your goals.

PART II

POSES
for
STRENGTH
and
FLEXIBILITY

HIPS AND THIGHS

YOUR HIPS AND LEGS are the drivetrain of your running stride. The stability of your hips and the mobility of your legs combine to move you over the ground. To that end, you need strength and flexibility in both the hips and the thighs to run well and avoid injury. Yoga offers a host of exercises that build both.

Standing Poses: Strength and Flexibility

Nowhere in the catalog of yoga asanas do the twin qualities of *sthira* and *sukha*— stability and mobility, strength and flexibility—shine more than in the standing poses. Moving in and out of the poses requires and builds isotonic strength, and holding them provides isometric exercise. When you flow from pose to pose, use the breath— generally, inhale to lift, exhale to lower. When you hold, allow the breath to come and go freely. Along the way, you gain flexibility and resilience through your legs.

WARRIOR I

WHY: Warrior I (Fig. 4.1) builds balanced strength in the muscles that act on the knee of the front leg while creating flexibility in the back-leg hip flexors and in the lower leg.

HOW: Standing tall, step forward with your left leg and angle your right heel in slightly. Pointing your pelvis straight ahead, inhale and lift your arms. Exhaling, lunge your left knee toward 90 degrees.

VARIATIONS: The width and length between your feet can confer stability or challenge your balance. Change your stance until you find what's right for you.

If you feel stress in your back knee, lift the heel and roll to the ball of the back foot.

Your arm position can change here: Arms can be parallel or hands can touch; elbows can bend; hands can clasp behind your back.

4.1 *Warrior I*

WARRIOR II

WHY: Like warrior I, warrior II (Fig. 4.2) supports knee health; at the same time, it increases flexibility in the inner thighs.

HOW: Take a wide stance, left toes turned out, right toes facing right. Inhale and lift your arms parallel to the floor; exhaling, lunge your left knee over your toes. Keep shoulders and pelvis stacked and squared to the long side of the mat, and turn just your head to look over your left hand.

VARIATIONS: Tight hips can make a proper lunge difficult. If your left knee is moving to the right, shorten your stance.

Add a side stretch to the pose by coming to exalted warrior (Fig. 4.3): Lift your front arm to the sky as you relax your back arm toward the ground.

4.2 *Warrior II*

4.3 *Exalted warrior*

WARRIOR III

WHY: Warrior III (Fig. 4.4) builds strength in the glutes and other hip stabilizers while stretching the back of the standing leg. It requires stability through the core and a focused sense of balance.

HOW: Stand tall and shift your weight onto your right leg. Hold shoulders, core, hips, and left leg in a long line as you hinge the pelvis forward and lift the left leg behind you.

VARIATIONS: Coming into and out of the pose with the breath makes a good dynamic warmup and workout for the hip muscles. Alternatively, holding the pose for a number of breaths is a good core challenge.

To increase or decrease intensity, change the position of your arms. Hands can reach back in an inverted *V,* off to the sides, or overhead for more work. Try holding hands in prayer position or interlacing your fingers behind your back to stretch your chest.

4.4 Warrior III

TRIANGLE

WHY: Triangle (Fig. 4.5) stretches the hamstrings and inner thigh on the front leg, the outer hip and calf on the back leg, and the torso and chest.

HOW: From a wide stance, turn your left toes out and angle your right foot roughly 90 degrees relative to the left. Keeping your spine long, extend it over your left leg as you rest your left hand on your thigh, shin, or ankle. Reach your right arm upward.

VARIATIONS: Use a block on either side of your left leg to rest your hand or go hands-free for a strength challenge.

Experiment to determine the best position for your hips. Rolling your right hip forward and pulling your left hip to the right slightly may allow your hip to stretch more.

Choose a position for your neck and head that works for you. You can look down, forward, or up.

4.5 *Triangle*

SIDE ANGLE

WHY: Like warrior II, side angle (Fig. 4.6) offers an inner-thigh stretch while building strength isometrically. It also stretches the entire side of the body and the chest.

HOW: From triangle pose, bend your left knee and rest your left elbow on your left thigh. Take your right arm by your head, creating a diagonal line from the right heel through the right hand.

VARIATIONS: For a deeper stretch, take your left hand to a block or to the floor, either inside or outside your left foot.

To stretch the chest more, lay your right forearm on your lower back, tucking the right fingers between the waist and left thigh.

4.6 Side angle

PYRAMID

WHY: Pyramid pose provides a deep hamstring and hip stretch for the front leg, a calf stretch for the back leg, and either a core challenge or a release for the back, depending on whether you hold your back actively (Fig. 4.7) or passively (Fig. 4.8).

HOW: From mountain pose, take a moderate step forward with your left leg. Angle your right heel in slightly. Keeping hips facing forward, fold your pelvis until you feel a hamstring stretch.

VARIATIONS: To work your core, hold your spine parallel to the floor. For more of a stretch, let your back arc over your front leg.

For challenge in the core work, take your arms to the sides or overhead. For release in the stretch, hands can rest on the front thigh, the shin, blocks, or the floor.

4.7 Pyramid with active back

4.8 Pyramid with passive back

RISHI FOLD

WHY: Rishi fold (Fig. 4.9) stretches the outer hamstrings, outer hip, and the IT band that connects them.

HOW: From mountain pose, take a short step forward with your right foot and align your left foot about 45 degrees relative to the right foot. Turn your pelvis to square it over the right leg, then fold forward.

VARIATIONS: Experiment with the position of your feet and your arms to find the best combination of stretch for you. Add a chest stretch by taking the hands together behind your back, then lifting them up.

4.9 Rishi fold

Lunges

Lunges are one of the most useful exercises for runners and can be approached as a strength-building or flexibility-building practice, depending on the position taken and the amount of time they are held. Echoing the leg position of warrior I, lunges evoke the split stance of the running stride.

HIGH LUNGE

WHY: High lunge (Fig. 4.10), like warrior I, builds strength in the legs while stretching the front-leg hamstrings and the back-leg hip flexors.

HOW: Take a stance with your left knee over your left ankle and your right leg long.

VARIATIONS: The position of your torso and hands affects the intensity and strength/flexibility demand here. Resting your hands on the floor increases the stretch in your front leg, while holding your hands to the front thigh requires more strength. Taking your arms overhead challenges your balance while deepening the stretch in your back leg.

Experiment with the alignment of your pelvis. Keeping your hips squared forward, bend your back knee, scoop your tailbone under, and then slowly straighten the back leg again.

4.10 *High lunge*

LOW LUNGE

WHY: Lunging with the back knee down (Fig. 4.11) gives you more stretch in the back leg.

HOW: From high lunge, lower your back knee to the ground, padding it with a towel or blanket if necessary. You can keep your back toes on the ground or rest on the top of the back foot.

VARIATIONS: As with high lunge, you can keep your hands low, take them to the knee, or raise them overhead.

As your hips release, try sliding the back knee further back. Doing so relieves pressure on the knee as well.

To add a quadriceps stretch, reach the hand of the back-leg side to the foot of that leg.

4.11 *Low lunge*

TWISTING LUNGE

WHY: Adding a twist to the lunge (Fig. 4.12) helps you gain and maintain mobility in the spine, stretches the chest, and builds flexibility in the hip.

HOW: From high or low lunge with the right leg forward, place your left hand on the floor under your left shoulder and the right hand on the right knee. Keeping your spine long, twist to look up over your right shoulder.

VARIATIONS: If you feel steady in the twist, take your right hand toward the ceiling.

For a greater challenge, work the left elbow to the outside of the right knee and stack the hands in prayer position.

To add a quadriceps stretch, reach the hand of the front-leg side around your back to reach the foot of the other leg.

4.12 *Twisting lunge*

LIZARD LUNGE

WHY: Moving the front leg wider to the side and placing the hands on the inside of the leg (Fig. 4.13) stretches the inner thigh and—depending on your individual anatomy—the outer hip while intensifying the stretch for the back-leg hip flexors.

HOW: From low lunge, walk both hands inside the front foot, while moving it closer to the outside of the mat. Stay on your hands or lower your elbows to a bolster, block, or the floor.

VARIATIONS: For more intensity, lift the back-leg knee off the floor.

　　To add a side stretch, walk both hands away from the forward leg.

4.13 *Lizard lunge*

RUNNER'S LUNGE

WHY: Runner's lunge stretches the hamstrings of the front leg.

HOW: From low lunge, shift your hips back as though standing on the back leg.

VARIATIONS: Pointing the toe stretches the top of the ankle (Fig. 4.14), while rolling back to the front heel works the calf muscles (Fig. 4.15).

For less intensity, place blocks underneath your hands and experiment to find the correct amount of bend in the front knee.

4.14 *Runner's lunge with ankle stretch*

4.15 *Runner's lunge with calf stretch*

Forward Folds

These poses target flexibility around the outer hips and hamstrings, common problem areas for runners. Combine them with lunges and backbends to stretch the front of the hips, so you can bring the complementary muscles into balance.

Changing your orientation to gravity will change the intensity of the stretch and the effects of the pose on your legs versus your back.

TIGHT FORWARD FOLD

WHY: In a tight forward fold, the stretch is centered in the central hamstrings. Longer holds of this pose (10 to 20 breaths) allow you to counteract some of the tightness your running incurs.

HOW: Keep your feet close together and your toes facing forward as you tilt from the pelvis (not hinge from the waist). Rest your hands anywhere on your legs—you need not reach your feet.

VARIATIONS: In a standing forward fold (Fig. 4.16), you'll feel gravity help release the back of your body. Your head and neck can let go. Bend your knees as much as you need to.

4.16 *Standing forward fold*

In the seated forward fold, you may need to add support, such as a rolled towel or blanket, under your knees if your hamstrings are very tight. Come into the pose with a long back to ensure you angle from the pelvis (Fig. 4.17), then allow your back to relax into the stretch (Fig. 4.18).

4.17 *Seated forward fold, beginning*

4.18 *Seated forward fold, end*

WIDE FORWARD FOLD

WHY: Taking your legs into a straddle changes the area affected by the forward fold, moving it into your inner hamstrings and inner thighs.

HOW: Move your legs as far apart as feels reasonable and fold from your pelvis.

VARIATIONS: In the standing straddle (Fig. 4.19), you can choose to walk your hands forward, keep them in line with your toes, or take them between your legs, fingers facing backward, for a deeper back stretch.

In either the standing or the seated version of this wide forward fold, you can move the hands toward one leg to shift the stretch (Fig. 4.20).

4.19 *Wide forward fold, standing straddle*

4.20 *Wide forward fold, shift to one side*

COW-FACE

WHY: This cross-legged fold (Fig. 4.21) relieves tightness in the outer hip and IT band, a common problem area for runners.

HOW: Sit cross-legged. This may be your starting point for the fold. If you can comfortably work one ankle over the opposite knee, do so; if you can cinch the knees together in front of your belly, do that. Wherever you wind up, fold forward until you feel a pleasant stretch.

VARIATIONS: If sitting on the ground makes you feel like you're slumped, elevate your hips on a block, firm pillow, or folded blanket.

If this pose is too intense, try it on your back (Fig. 4.22). Lie down and pull your crossed legs toward your chest, holding your shins or your ankles.

4.21 *Cow-face*

4.22 *Reclining cow-face*

PIGEON FORWARD FOLD

WHY: Folding forward in pigeon pose (Fig. 4.23) provides a strong stretch for the outer hip, including the glutes, the deeper hip rotators such as the piriformis, and the IT band. This pose, and its many variations, is one of the most useful for runners.

HOW: From table position, on your hands and knees, place your left knee behind your left hand and your left foot in front of your right hip. Lower your hips and fold your torso toward the ground, sliding your arms forward and resting on your palms, forearms, or lower.

VARIATIONS: Pigeon can feel too intense in the hips or strain the knee. To ease the pressure, lower your left hip to the ground and bend your right knee. Or add padding under your pelvis so that less weight is dropped into the stretch.

Finding a new orientation can customize the degree of stretch, too. A standing version of pigeon (Fig. 4.24) allows you to carefully control the amount of weight you put into the bent, stretching leg. From standing, cross your right ankle above your left knee and bend the left leg.

For a change of focus, do the pose on your back (Fig. 4.25). You can hold your supporting-leg shin or thigh; keep your shoulders and neck relaxed. Or try the pose at the wall, with the supporting leg propped against it. From there, you can deepen the stretch by bending that knee and sliding the foot down the wall.

4.23 *Pigeon forward fold*

4.25 *Reclining pigeon*

4.24 *Standing pigeon*

PIGEON BACKBEND

WHY: While technically a fold only for the front leg, pigeon backbend (Fig. 4.26) continues the stretch of the forward fold while increasing flexibility in the front of the back-leg hip, the muscles of the belly, and the chest.

HOW: From pigeon forward fold, lift your torso and rest your hands on the floor, your legs, or your hips. Pull the front knee back slightly and the back leg forward. Lift your chest into a light backbend.

VARIATIONS: If you are very engaged in the legs, you may not need your arms to hold you up; take them to your hips.

To add a quadriceps stretch (Fig. 4.27), roll off the kneecap onto the base of the back-leg thigh, reaching for your foot with one or both hands.

4.26 *Pigeon backbend*

4.27 *Pigeon backbend with quadriceps stretch*

HEAD-TO-KNEE

WHY: The asymmetrical head-to-knee fold (Fig. 4.28) focuses on one leg at a time while stretching the muscles that connect your pelvis and spine and that run up the length of your back.

HOW: From sitting, extend your right leg and bend the left, taking the sole of the left foot against the inner thigh of the right leg. Fold forward over the leg, resting your left hand on the inner edge of the right thigh, shin, or foot.

VARIATIONS: You can emphasize the slight twist here by keeping your right hand propped on the floor and looking over the right shoulder.

The placement of your left knee will affect the stretch for your back. If your knee is hovering in space, support it on a block or blanket. To stretch your back more, try sliding the left knee a few inches back and to the left.

4.28 *Head-to-knee*

REVOLVED HEAD-TO-KNEE

WHY: The revolved version of head-to-knee (Fig. 4.29) stretches the inner thigh and sets the pelvis and spine into a position that allows a great release in the side waist and back.

HOW: From head-to-knee with the right leg long, orient your belly to face over the bent left knee. Take your right hand to the inner right thigh and open your left arm wide. Slide into a side bend, reaching the left arm overhead or over the right leg until you find a good stretch for the back.

VARIATIONS: You need not move into the side bend; if you feel an inner thigh and back stretch as you sit upright, stay there and breathe.

To stretch the left side of the chest, sit tall and wrap your left forearm behind your lower back, reaching the left fingers for the right hip crease.

4.29 *Revolved head-to-knee*

Twists

These twisting poses add a hip stretch to the twist for the spine and stretch for the chest, making a great multitasking pose. Twists increase the range of motion through the spine.

HALF LORD OF THE FISHES/LORD OF THE FISHES

WHY: These twists help you hold your spine long against gravity, as you do when you run. Twisting strengthens the muscles that support the spine, even as it twists. In addition, you'll stretch your outer hip and chest.

4.30 *Half Lord of the Fishes*

HOW: From sitting, take the sole of the right foot across the left thigh. For half Lord of the Fishes (Fig. 4.30), the left leg is bent at the knee, with the left foot by the right hip; for Lord of the Fishes (Fig. 4.31), the left leg is straight. Sitting tall, place your right hand on the floor or a block by your right hip, and hold your right knee with your left hand.

VARIATION: For more twist, take the inner or outer left elbow to the outside of the right knee.

4.31 *Lord of the Fishes*

RECLINING HALF LORD OF THE FISHES

WHY: Reclining half Lord of the Fishes (Fig. 4.32) stretches your outer hip and thighs while lightening the intensity of the twist.

HOW: Lie on your back, left knee bent toward the ceiling, left foot to the right of the right thigh, right knee bent and right heel by the left hip.

VARIATIONS: If your flexibility or arm length permits, hold your ankles.

To increase the stretch in the front of the right hip, rest the left foot on the right thigh.

For a different approach, straighten your right leg, as for Lord of the Fishes.

4.32 *Reclining half Lord of the Fishes*

CROSS-LEGGED RECLINING TWIST

WHY: Cross-legged reclining twist (Fig. 4.33) offers a deep stretch for the outer hip and a pleasant twist for the spine while the chest relaxes toward the floor.

HOW: Lie on your back, left knee crossed tightly over the right. Drop both knees to the right and spread your arms to your sides.

VARIATIONS: If this feels too intense, uncross your legs and stack your knees (Fig. 4.34), or cross the left leg over with the right leg extending straight toward the bottom of the mat (Fig. 4.35).

Experiment with arm position; you may take the right hand to the left knee and the left arm almost overhead, to stretch the chest.

4.33 *Cross-legged reclining twist*

4.34 *Reclining twist with stacked knees*

4.35 *Reclining twist with straight leg*

Strap Stretches

To address tightness in your hamstrings and hips in depth, use a strap for reclining stretches. The floor holds your back in a relatively neutral position, and working one leg at a time allows you to pay attention to each layer of sensation and each muscle in your thigh.

HAMSTRINGS

WHY: While tension in your hamstrings can be good for your running, helping with efficient energy transfer, too much tension will create a host of problems, including back pain, hip pain, and pain in the lower leg. Stretching this muscle group carefully will help you maintain a fluid stride.

HOW: Lie on your back with your left knee bent and the strap around the ball of the right foot. Slowly reach the sole of the right foot toward the ceiling, keeping your shoulders, neck, and head relaxed.

VARIATION: For more intensity, slide your left leg long (Fig. 4.36).

4.36 *Hamstring stretch with leg extended*

You can work to stretch each of your hamstring muscles by moving the position of your leg a few inches in either direction. To stretch your outer hamstrings, which interface with your IT band, move your right leg over the left side of your body while keeping your right hip down (Fig. 4.37). To stretch your inner hamstrings, which interface with your adductors (inner thigh muscles), keep your pelvis steady and slide your right foot toward the right a few inches (Fig. 4.38).

4.37 *Hamstring stretch with leg moved inward*

4.38 *Hamstring stretch with leg moved outward*

INNER THIGH

WHY: The inner thigh stretch (Fig. 4.39) is different from the inner hamstring stretch, as it takes the leg much wider. Maintaining balance in strength and flexibility between the inner and outer sides of the thighs is important for injury prevention.

HOW: With the right hand, hold the strap snug around the ball of the foot. Keeping the pelvis level against the floor, drop your right leg to the right.

VARIATIONS: If this is too strong a stretch, bend your right knee and take the sole of the right foot toward the ceiling in a half happy baby stretch (Fig. 4.40). Or support the right leg from below with cushions.

4.39 *Inner thigh stretch*

4.40 *Half happy baby stretch*

OUTER THIGH AND HIP

WHY: The outer hip and IT band can become woefully tight on runners. Maintaining some flexibility down the outside of your leg keeps your stride fluid and prevents injury.

HOW: Hold the strap around the right foot in your left hand. With your left leg long, drop your right leg to the left, either letting it hover or resting it on the floor. Reach your right arm straight out (Fig. 4.41). Gaze over your right shoulder.

VARIATIONS: Bend your right knee to make the stretch less intense.

To focus on your hips, work the pelvis toward perpendicular with the floor. To stretch your back and chest more, let your pelvis angle and keep your right shoulder down on the ground.

4.41 *Outer thigh and hip stretch*

5

CORE

A STABLE CORE is key to good running form and injury avoidance, and its importance cannot be overestimated. Your core is the musculature of your trunk and pelvis. This includes your abdominal muscles, comprised of the superficial "six pack" (actually, an eight pack) of the rectus abdominis as well as the deeper muscles of the external and internal obliques and the transversus abdominis. It also includes the many layers of muscles that support your spine and connect it to your pelvis. That group contains not only the erector spinae muscles but also the muscles that attach your spine to parts of your lower body, such as the psoas and quadratus lumborum.

Also critical to stable core function are the muscles of the pelvic floor, which constitute the basement of the core, and the diaphragm, which bisects it and which aids in core stability. Yoga practice builds both of these groups. The pelvic floor creates the action of *mula bandha,* or the "root lock," which lightly engages and lifts the muscles at the bottom of your pelvis, conferring stability and tone. And yoga's approach to breathing exercises will strengthen your diaphragm and give you new access to the diaphragm's support for your spine.

Each of the muscle groups of the core must be both strong and resilient so that you can maintain good form both through a single running stride and over the course of a run. If you have weak abdominal muscles, you'll wiggle with each step, irritating the muscles of the hip and the iliotibial band and causing a reaction up and down the kinetic chain. Weak back muscles will fail to hold you erect when you tire, leading to hunching that restricts your breathing. A poorly functioning quadratus lumborum or psoas negatively affects the relationship between your pelvis and spine, causing trouble around the lower back and hips.

Yoga's approach to core strength combines stability and mobility. Some poses require you to hold yourself still in space, using the muscles of the belly and back to stabilize you. Building on strength developed in stillness, you can challenge your core muscles to stabilize you even as your limbs are moving. This is the central function of the core during the running stride: Your core must remain stable even as your limbs are moving in space. Other yoga exercises target the smaller, deeper muscles that control the movements of the spine, demanding that you mobilize the joints in the spine as you move in space. This mobility helps you maintain full function in the spine, which is critical for injury prevention. This distinction between stability and mobility exercises echoes the principle of *sthira* and *sukha* we explored in Chapter 1. We need both firmness and softness, stability and mobility, for optimal health.

As you try the poses described here, be sure you don't hold your breath. Instead, breathe fully and deeply. If it's tough to breathe, try a variation that will help you build strength; after a few weeks, you'll be able to make it harder. How many breaths you hold the static poses, or how many rounds of the dynamic poses you complete, is up to you. A good rule of thumb is to work to pleasant fatigue. Depending on the exercise, 5 breaths might suffice, or 15—listen to your body (not your ego) to learn what the right challenge is for you.

Planks

In plank positions, you are working to build stability and hold your core steady in space. Planks can be done on hands, elbows, or a prop; your knees or your feet; and in various relationships to gravity. Whichever variation you choose, remember your mountain pose alignment. Hold your legs steady and your pelvis neutral, including a light lift along the bottom of your pelvis. Engage your belly and keep your lower ribs moving toward your spine, but make sure you have room to breathe. Let your shoulder blades descend. Keep your neck long and your chin low.

PLANK

WHY: Taking plank face down challenges your core muscles to work against gravity. Practiced with good alignment, it stabilizes your shoulders, helping you keep your shoulder blades neutral and upper body relaxed as you run.

HOW: From your hands and knees, turn the balls of your feet to the ground and straighten your legs. You may need to slide your feet back. Hold your shoulders over your wrists, spreading your fingers wide and making lots of contact between the palms and fingers and the floor (Fig. 5.1).

5.1 *Plank*

VARIATIONS: To lighten any strain on your back, drop your knees to the ground.

For more challenge, try picking up one foot, then the other, mimicking the single-leg stance of the running stride. For still more work, try also lifting the opposite arm as you walk your feet (Fig. 5.2). You can also pulse in and out of plank pose from downward-facing dog (Fig. 5.3). Inhale to plank; exhale to downward-facing dog (also called "down dog").

5.2 *Plank with opposite arm and leg lifted*

5.3 *Downward-facing dog*

ARROWHEAD PLANK

WHY: Arrowhead plank (Fig. 5.4), done on your forearms, challenges the muscles of the core more directly by removing arm and, to a great degree, chest strength from the equation. As with plank on your palms, arrowhead helps build shoulder integrity.

HOW: Come into plank pose with the forearms on the ground. Elbows align under shoulders. Hands can meet in prayer position, interlace at the fingers, or rest sphinx-style in front of the elbows.

VARIATIONS: Drop your knees to lighten the workload.

For more work, lift and lower a leg, an arm, or opposite leg and arm.

To flow from one position to the other, move from arrowhead plank to a full straight-armed plank, walking first one, then the other arm up before returning both to the ground. Or, move from arrowhead plank on an exhalation into dolphin pose (Fig. 5.5), which is downward-facing dog on the forearms. Be advised that this is quite a strong hamstring and shoulder stretch! The pulse between poses challenges your muscles in new ways and can serve as a nice warm-up before you hold the pose for any length of time.

5.4 *Arrowhead plank*

5.5 *Dolphin*

CHATURANGA

WHY: This variation of plank, hovering off the floor with elbows bent to 90 degrees (Fig. 5.6), requires and builds full-body strength. *Chaturanga* is an advanced move that requires supreme control. It's taught in many yoga classes, even classes for beginners, and you may be invited to practice it sooner than you are ready. You may modify your *chaturanga* by dropping your knees or skipping the pose entirely until you feel ready.

HOW: From a straight-armed plank, shift your weight forward a few inches, then, exhaling, bend elbows to 90 degrees. Keep your upper arms close to your body and your shoulders at the level of your elbows. Dipping them lower can strain the front of the shoulders excessively.

VARIATIONS: Drop your knees to modify.

For more intensity, do pushups from *chaturanga* back to plank. Or lower an inch, then hover for the inhalation; lower another inch, then hover, until you reach the 90-degree bend at the front of the elbows.

5.6 Chaturanga

SIDE PLANK

WHY: Turning your plank in relationship to gravity challenges the stabilizing muscles in your hips. These are critical for proper running form. Being strong in your hips helps prevent a host of running injuries. Further, balancing on one arm builds upper body strength and improves your sense of whole-body balance.

HOW: From a downward-facing plank pose, pivot onto the right arm and the outer edge of the right foot, stacking the left foot on top of the right (Fig. 5.7). Keep your right ankle flexed to 90 degrees and your hips high. Your left hand can be on your hip or in the air. Gaze straight forward or up toward the sky.

VARIATIONS: Leg position greatly affects the intensity of the side plank. For less intensity, practice on the right knee with the left foot resting on the ground. For slightly more, stay straight in the right leg but rest the left foot on the ground in front of the right shin or knee. For still more intensity, lift your left leg up and let it hover, or rest your left foot on your right shin or inner thigh for tree pose in side plank. Dropping to the forearm (Fig. 5.8) will alleviate strain on the wrist while building shoulder stability.

5.7 *Side plank*

Another option is keeping your legs stacked but bending both knees, so that knees, hips, and shoulders are in line as the shins run parallel to the short side of your mat (Fig. 5.9). This is a good way to target hip strength and shoulder stability, especially if you slowly lift and lower your bottom hip to the floor.

5.8 *Side plank on forearm*

5.9 *Side plank on knees*

REVERSE PLANK

WHY: Reverse plank (Fig. 5.10) stretches the entire front side of your body as it strengthens the entire back side. You'll release the muscles of your chest and belly, as well as your hip flexors and ankles, in a full reverse plank. These areas can grow excessively tight on runners. Meanwhile, your back muscles and hamstrings will have to work to hold you up.

HOW: From a sitting position, with hands by the hips and fingers forward, lift your chest through your shoulders. Then push into your hands to lift your hips up. Try to keep your toes on the floor. Choose a position for your neck and head that is relaxing.

VARIATIONS: Bending the knees to 90 degrees, with feet directly underneath, lessens the workload. This is often called reverse table pose (Fig. 5.11).

Holding the core steady while lifting, then lowering one leg at a time challenges the muscles of the core to hold steady while you run. This can be done whether you are in full reverse plank or reverse table pose (Fig. 5.12).

5.10 *Reverse plank*

5.11 *Reverse table*

5.12 *Reverse table with leg lifted*

Boats

Boat pose and its variations take the plank position and break it at the hips. This enables you to build strength through the core and hip flexors while balancing your body in space. There are almost infinite ways to vary the position of your legs and arms, making this pose both immediately accessible and vastly customizable.

BOAT

WHY: Boat (Fig. 5.13) challenges your balance while working your core.

HOW: Sit with your knees bent and hands on your hamstrings. Lean back while keeping your torso long and chest open. Lift your shins toward parallel with the ground.

VARIATIONS: For less intensity, keep your feet on the floor.

For more intensity, hold your arms parallel to the ground. Next, straighten your legs (Fig. 5.14). Then, you can hold your arms parallel to your legs or overhead, forming an open *V* (Fig. 5.15). Choose the variation that challenges you while still allowing you to breathe.

5.13 *Boat*

5.14 *Boat with extended legs*

5.15 *Boat with extended arms and legs*

BOAT WITH A TWIST

WHY: Twisting from boat works your obliques, the abdominal muscles that control the light twist that occurs in your running stride as each leg moves from front to back.

HOW: From boat, take your hands together in prayer position. Inhaling, turn to the right (Fig. 5.16) and lower the right elbow toward the floor. Exhaling, return to center. Repeat on the other side.

VARIATIONS: Choose a lower leg position, or keep your feet on the ground, to make the twist easier. Or, for a different approach, twist your feet, too, bending at the knees and swinging your feet toward the left hip as you twist to the right.

5.16 *Boat with a twist*

BOAT TO HALF BOAT

WHY: Lifting and lowering in and out of boat pose increases the challenge and hones your control over your core.

HOW: From boat, inhale and lower your back and legs toward the ground (Fig. 5.17). As you exhale, return to boat.

VARIATIONS: This action can be subtle, especially if you hold your torso in boat but lower only your feet, knees bent. Or it can be dramatic, if you lower your back almost all the way down, arms swept overhead and legs hovering an inch from the mat.

5.17 *Half boat*

Back Extension Exercises

Back extension exercises help build strength in the muscles of the upper back. When these muscles are weak, it's easy to round into a hunch toward the end of a hard or long run. When they are strong, you'll be able to hold your chest open while running, as well as during daily activities such as driving, keyboarding, or sitting in a chair. An upright, open posture makes more room for full breaths and is less taxing for the muscles of your back. The chest stretch provided by these poses complements the goal of having a strong back and a flexible front.

BIRD DOG

WHY: The bird dog (Fig. 5.18) requires your back muscles to support your spine as your arms and legs move contralaterally. This is exactly what happens during the running stride.

HOW: From table position on your hands and knees, hold your pelvis and spine in a neutral line. Extend your right arm forward and your left leg back while maintaining this neutral position in your core. Then change sides.

5.18 *Bird dog*

VARIATIONS: Try pulsing with the breath, inhaling to extend your arm and opposite leg and exhaling to return them to the ground.

For more challenge, include spinal extension and flexion. As you inhale, lift your arm and opposite leg higher into a slight backbend (Fig. 5.19). Exhaling, bend your knee and elbow and draw them toward each other as you round your back (Fig. 5.20). Do 5, 10, or 15 rounds before moving to the other side.

5.19 *Bird dog with backbend*

5.20 *Bird dog with rounded back*

COBRA

WHY: Cobra (Fig. 5.21) stretches the chest while engaging the muscles of the back, helping you fight against the late-run hunched-over position.

HOW: While lying on your belly, spread your hands beneath your shoulders. Pushing into your palms, pull your elbows back and your chest forward as you lift your upper body into a backbend.

VARIATIONS: Trying staying close to the ground and lifting the hands off the mat to ensure you're engaging your back to lift. Or, push higher into the backbend while still keeping your hips down.

5.21 *Cobra*

UPWARD-FACING DOG

WHY: Upward-facing dog (Fig. 5.22), often called "up dog," is a continuation of the action of cobra pose. Since the hips are lifted off the ground, it offers a stretch for the hip flexors in addition to the chest opening of cobra.

HOW: From cobra pose, straighten your arms completely. Shoulders, which should be over wrists, stay broad as your chest opens. Keep the leg muscles engaged as you rest on the tops of your feet.

VARIATIONS: If your chest is tight, make it easier by resting on the knees or thighs instead of the feet.

Upward-facing dog is usually practiced as part of a sequence that moves from plank to *chaturanga* to upward-facing dog to downward-facing dog. You can also flow back and forth from up dog to down dog. Either way, the movement into upward-facing dog comes on an inhalation. You'll find this sequence in the sun salutations routine in Chapter 15.

5.22 *Upward-facing dog*

LOCUST

WHY: Locust (Fig. 5.23) helps strengthen the entire back side of the body, targeting the erector spinae as well as the serratus and rhomboids. These muscles help you maintain good shoulder position as you run. Locust also builds hamstring strength, which can help correct an imbalance between the hip flexors and the hamstrings.

HOW: Lie on your belly, hands by your hips. Engage the whole back of your body to lift your chest and legs from the floor. You can inhale to lift and exhale to lower or choose to remain in the pose for a number of breaths.

VARIATIONS: For a deeper chest stretch, interlace your hands behind your back or hold a strap. For more challenge for the shoulders and arms, extend your arms overhead (Fig. 5.24).

5.23 *Locust*

5.24 *Locust with arms extended*

BOW

WHY: Bow pose (Fig. 5.25) takes the action of locust—the engagement of the entire back side of the body—and further stretches the front side of the body by forging a connection between the hands and feet.

HOW: Lie on your belly and bend your knees. Reach your hands to your feet. Inhaling, push into the hips and kick your feet into your hands as you rise into the backbend. Keep your neck relaxed.

5.25 *Bow*

VARIATIONS: A half bow (Fig. 5.26) is a good choice if you are having trouble reaching both feet simultaneously. Or use a strap to help connect hands and feet.

To work both sides of the back from half bow, lift the right side of the body into locust pose while the left is in half bow (Fig. 5.27).

5.26 *Half bow*

5.27 *Locust/bow*

Articulations

In these exercises, you'll work to stabilize one part of your body and mobilize another. Focus on detailed control while performing these asanas. The slower you can move, the better you'll access the small, deep muscles in your back. These exercises can be repeated for a total of 5 breaths, 10 breaths, or more.

ROLL-DOWN/ROLL-UP

WHY: The roll-down and roll-up use the abdominal muscles to control your ascent and descent and the back muscles to straighten yourself as you rise. This articulation targets the small muscles that work in harmony to move and to support your spine; you want these strong to keep you running tall.

HOW: Sit with knees bent and hands on your hamstrings. On an exhalation, keeping feet on the ground, scoop your tailbone under and begin a slow roll-down (Fig. 5.28) until your back is on the ground. Inhaling, bring your chin to your chest and roll yourself all the way up.

VARIATIONS: Holding your hands to your thighs gives you some leverage for the trip back up to sitting. You can also push your elbows into the ground if you need an extra lift.

To add challenge, try the roll-down and roll-up with legs straight. For still more work, change your center of gravity by extending your arms overhead.

5.28 *Roll-down/roll-up*

LEG LIFT

WHY: Leg lifts require you to hold your core stable as you move your legs against gravity. They work all areas of your core musculature—including the hip flexors, critical for pulling your leg up while you run.

HOW: Lie on your back, knees bent, palms to the floor beside your hips. Inhale and slowly move your knees into the space above your hips. Exhale and, holding your core steady, lower your feet back to the ground.

VARIATIONS: Moving one leg at a time lessens the strain on your back while allowing you to pay close attention to controlling this motion.

For more challenge, work with straight legs (Fig. 5.29). For still more, take the arms out to a *T* or overhead.

5.29 *Leg lift*

OBLIQUE TWIST

WHY: Similar to twisting from boat pose, twisting on your back works your obliques. You'll have to stabilize from the center even as your legs are moving, just as you do when you run.

HOW: Resting on your back, knees bent over your hips, take your arms to a *T* position. Keeping your shoulders on the floor, inhale and lower your knees toward the right. Exhale and return them to center before repeating on the left. (This breath pattern, different from the breath for leg lifts, ensures you exhale on exertion.) Your goal is to hold your legs just above the floor while keeping your shoulders on the floor (Fig. 5.30).

VARIATIONS: To make this easier, spread your knees and don't lower them as far.

To make it harder, work with straight legs spread wide. To make it harder still, work with straight legs together. Adding an extra breath with the legs to the side also increases the difficulty of the pose.

5.30 *Oblique twist*

BRIDGE ARTICULATIONS

WHY: Moving in and out of bridge pose works the back of the body—the muscles along the spine as well as the glutes and hamstrings—as it stretches the front, especially chest, belly, hip flexors, and quadriceps. This helps the front of the body remain in balance with the back.

HOW: Rest on your back with your hands by your hips, feet directly under bent knees. Inhale and press into your feet to lift your hips up (Fig. 5.31). Exhale and slowly lower from the top to the bottom of your spine.

VARIATIONS: Holding at the top of bridge pose offers a different approach; you can walk your shoulder blades toward each other and keep your hands on the floor or interlace your fingers (Fig. 5.32).

5.31 *Bridge*

To change the effect of the articulation to bridge, try using your arms, too. On an inhalation, sweep your arms overhead to the floor (Fig. 5.33); as you exhale, lower them back by your hips.

5.32 *Bridge using arms*

5.33 *Bridge with hands on floor*

Pelvic Floor

Maintaining tone in the muscles of the pelvic floor provides a stable base for your core. Additionally, it helps you maintain integrity even with the impact of running, which bounces your abdominal organs with each step. If you've suffered from running-related incontinence (a fairly common occurrence, especially in women who are mothers), you know it's no fun. Paying attention to engaging the muscles of the pelvic floor will lighten this discomfort.

ROOT LOCK

WHY: The root lock is a light engagement and lift of the muscles of the pelvic floor. It helps contain energy in the core, rather than letting it leak out toward the ground.

HOW: Engage the muscles of your perineum. This action can enhance any pose, especially those where you spread your legs wide and those where you squat.

VARIATIONS: If you're finding the root lock hard to achieve, take a squatting position (Fig. 5.34) and start with a crude clench of the entire pelvic floor. At first, you may need to overdo this by clenching all the muscles in the area, as though you are trying to prevent yourself from elimination. Next, see if you can relax the work in the superficial muscles while maintaining the contraction a little deeper.

Notice how the root lock is affected by your breath. It lightens as you inhale and increases as you exhale. This slight pulse comes as a result of the pressure in your abdomen. Keeping a slight lift and lock helps support your core.

5.34 *Root lock*

6

LOWER LEGS

THE LOWER LEG plays a critical role in the running stride. As our point of contact with the ground, the foot—proportionally, a very small area—must transfer large amounts of energy. The elastic rebound of the calf muscles aids in this effort. When the lower legs aren't functioning correctly, either because of deconditioning, structural issues, or improper footwear choices, running becomes at best less efficient and at worst injurious.

As you practice the stretches outlined in this chapter, hold each for five or more breaths. The muscular stretch will finish after 30 to 60 seconds; longer holds can affect the fascia, the soft tissue that surrounds the muscles. Thus longer holds can effect slow, long-term change in the body.

Squatting Poses

As yoga teachers love to point out, many people in the Eastern world get by just fine without using chairs. Instead, they squat. Squatting releases the soft tissue around the lower back, an area criss-crossed by muscles, ligaments, and a thick sheaf of fascia. It also offers deep compression for the knees and ankles, which, practiced wisely, can retain healthy function in the joints. The trick is to avoid pain but not to shy away from longer holds. Here are some poses that can ensure you retain healthy function in your lower legs while also achieving a release for your back.

NARROW SQUAT

WHY: A narrow squat (Fig. 6.1) stretches your back, thighs, calves, and Achilles tendon.

HOW: Squat with your knees together inside your elbows.

VARIATIONS: If your heels do not reach the ground, use your hands to help you balance. You can even slowly shift your weight forward and back, to spread the stretch across your lower legs.

Find a nice release for your back by resting your belly over your thighs and dropping your chin into the space between your knees.

6.1 *Narrow squat*

TOE BALANCE

WHY: Balancing in a narrow squat on the balls of your feet (Fig. 6.2) strengthens the stabilizing muscles in your feet while stretching the soles.

HOW: From a narrow squat, shift your weight forward so your thighs are parallel to the ground. Balance your shoulders over your hips with your hands to your thighs.

VARIATIONS: For more challenge, take your hands to prayer position or overhead.

6.2 *Toe balance*

WIDE SQUAT

WHY: A wide squat position (Fig. 6.3) adds a groin stretch and may allow you to rest your heels on the floor. Depending on your bone structure and flexibility, you may prefer one version of the squat over the other.

HOW: Take your knees wide, letting them face out over your toes. Depending on your body, knees and toes may angle 45 degrees from the midline or not. Hands can rest on the floor, your thighs, or in prayer position with your elbows inside your knees.

VARIATION: If your heels don't reach the floor, you can add a blanket or towel underneath them.

6.3 *Wide squat*

Kneeling Poses

Kneeling brings your knees into even fuller flexion, and it offers a stretch for the shins, including the tibialis muscles, where irritation can lead to shin splints. Kneeling also releases the tops of the ankles. More range of motion in your ankles will allow for a more fluid running stride.

CHILD'S POSE

WHY: Child's pose (Fig. 6.4) offers a full-back release, as well as a grounding, settling place to pay attention to your breath. While you do, you'll stretch your lower back, quadriceps, shins, and ankles.

6.4 *Child's pose*

HOW: Kneel on a soft surface (you may need to add padding for your knees and shins), big toes close together, knees however wide you like. Fold forward so that your belly rests on your thighs, lowering your forehead toward the ground. Rest your hands alongside your feet.

VARIATIONS: If this is too extreme for your ankles, rest your shins on a stack of blankets so that the tops of your feet don't take too much pressure. If your hips won't settle toward your heels or you feel strain in your knees, slide a blanket between your calves and hamstrings.

For a different experience for your back, vary the width of your knees.

To stretch your shoulders, slide your arms long overhead, pushing your palms into the ground.

To stretch your chest, take your hands together behind your back and then raise them behind you (Fig. 6.5).

6.5 *Child's pose with raised hands*

ROCK

WHY: This kneeling position deepens the ankle stretch of child's pose by adding the weight of the torso.

HOW: Sit on your heels, with your knees close together and your hands on your thighs (Fig. 6.6).

VARIATIONS: If this is too much for your knees, slide a blanket between your calves and hamstrings to decrease the bend in your knees (Fig. 6.7).

To stretch your chest and to change the experience in your legs, take your hands behind you and lean back.

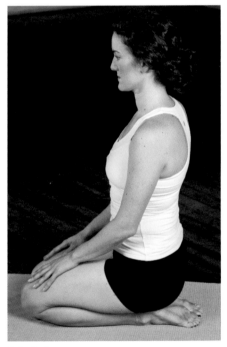

6.6 *Rock*

6.7 *Rock with blanket*

HERO

WHY: Hero pose (Fig. 6.8) stretches the quads more deeply while maintaining the ankle stretch of rock pose. Not every body can tolerate the internal rotation this pose requires of your legs, so skip it if you feel strain.

HOW: From kneeling, slide your knees and ankles wide and sit between your feet.

VARIATIONS: If your bottom doesn't reach the ground, slide some padding under your sitting bones.

Deepen the stretch for the front of the body by leaning back or even lying back (Fig. 6.9).

6.8 Hero

6.9 Reclining hero

Kneeling/Squatting Combinations

These hybrids combine the squatting and kneeling positions. They can help you multitask, and they challenge you in new ways.

TOE STRETCH

WHY: The toe stretch (Fig. 6.10) stretches not only the toes but the entire sole of the foot. It can give relief in the early stages of plantar fasciitis, an irritation of the connective tissue that runs from the heel across the arch. Practiced regularly, it can even ward off plantar fasciitis.

HOW: From a toe squat, drop your knees to the ground, or from kneeling, flip the balls of the feet to the floor. Sit on your heels and breathe.

VARIATION: It can be surprising how strong this stretch is. To lighten the intensity, lift your hips so you are standing on your knees.

6.10 *Toe stretch*

HALF KNEELING, HALF SQUAT

WHY: Positioning one leg in a squat and one kneeling (Fig. 6.11) allows you to notice and deepen the actions in one leg at a time.

HOW: From a kneeling position, take one leg up into a squat, knee and toes facing forward, heel on the ground.

VARIATIONS: To emphasize the stretch for the back of the squatting leg, lean the weight of your torso onto your thigh.

To stretch the kneeling-leg shin and ankle, place your hands under your shoulders and lift your kneeling-side knee as you stretch the front of the leg (Fig. 6.12).

6.11 *Half kneeling, half squat*

6.12 *Half kneeling, half squat with shin and ankle stretch*

7

UPPER BODY

AS YOU RUN, your upper body provides contralateral movement to balance the action of your lower body. That is, when one leg is forward, the opposite arm is back, and vice versa. All this action requires the integrity of a long spine and stable pelvis to be efficient. As we saw with the bird dog exercise in Chapter 5, it requires strong back and abdominal muscles. It also requires both strength and openness in the upper body: strength to help you flex your elbows and hold your shoulders steady and openness so that you can swing your arms without excessively twisting your shoulder girdle side to side.

Focus on breathing throughout each stretch. As you move through the shoulder circles, you can inhale to help lift your arms and exhale to settle your arms back toward the ground. When you twist, let the inhalations remind you to sit tall and the exhalations slide you deeper into rotation.

Strap Stretches

Strap stretches help you gain mobility in your shoulders and flexibility in your chest and arms. Yoga straps are available for purchase, or you can fashion your own using a belt or two, a long scarf, or a woven dog leash.

All these stretches can be done while standing, kneeling, sitting cross-legged—or even sitting in your desk chair.

SHOULDER CIRCLES

WHY: This comprehensive stretch works the entire musculature of your chest and upper back.

HOW: Hold your strap with your hands about shoulder distance apart. Lift your arms overhead and back until you feel a pleasant intensity (Fig. 7.1), then lower them. After a few rounds of this, spread your hands a little wider and take your arms farther back. Eventually, you can widen your grip so that your arms can reach behind your back to your waist.

VARIATIONS: You can flow with your breath, inhaling to lift your arms and exhaling to lower them. Or, move slower, investigating the experience of lifting and of staying at the edge of the intense stretch.

7.1 *Shoulder circles*

BICEPS AND TRICEPS STRETCH

WHY: This move stretches your upper arm and the front of your shoulder, freeing up range of motion for your arm swing in running.

HOW: With a wide grip on your strap, take your right arm overhead while the left reaches off to the side (Fig. 7.2) to stretch the left biceps. After 5 to 10 breaths, bend your right elbow and choke up on the strap to stretch the right triceps (Fig. 7.3). Be sure to do the same on the other side.

VARIATIONS: Try taking your left arm behind you slightly or rotate your left arm so that the palm faces up or down. You can experiment similarly with the placement of your right elbow to stretch the right arm.

7.2 *Biceps stretch*

7.3 *Triceps stretch*

Passive Backbends

Some active backbends—cobra, upward-facing dog, and bridge pose—were covered in Chapter 5 as back-extension core exercises. Here are some lovely complements to that work: passive backbends. These poses stretch your chest without requiring your back to work. They make good post-run stretches but also work as a way to unwind after spending the day sitting.

FISH ON A BOLSTER

WHY: Reclining with a pillow supporting your spine (Fig. 7.4), you'll enjoy a gentle stretch for the chest and shoulders. Practicing this position is a great way to grow still and quiet and to notice how your breath is moving.

HOW: Recline with a yoga bolster, a rolled blanket or towel, or a foam roller wrapped in a blanket under your spine. If you feel a strong curve in your lower back, push into your feet, lift your hips, and tuck your tailbone a little. Add a pillow for your neck if your chin is jutting up. Spread your arms to the sides and stay for a few minutes.

7.4 *Passive backbend*

VARIATIONS: How you position your legs affects your comfort. Options include bending the knees and propping them together with your feet slightly wider, stretching your legs long, or assuming cobbler pose, with the soles of the feet together and knees dropped to either side (support the knees on blankets or pillows for less intensity).

For more intensity, reposition the bolster to run perpendicular to your spine along your back ribs (Fig. 7.5).

7.5 *Passive backbend with bolster perpendicular to spine*

FISH ON BLOCKS

WHY: This version of the supported backbend is more intense than reclining on the bolster, meaning you can achieve release faster.

HOW: Use two yoga blocks to form a *T*: one block at medium height to form the base of the *T* and the other on the shortest side to form the crossbar. Lie back so that the base of the medium-height block rests between your shoulder blades and the tall block supports the back of your head (Fig. 7.6). You may need to sit up and reposition the blocks to find the best arrangement.

VARIATIONS: As with fish on a bolster, you have many choices about the position of your legs: experiment with straightening and bending the knees and with dropping them toward or away from each other.

If the blocks feel too high, flip each of them one level lower.

7.6 *Fish on blocks*

BRIDGE ON A BOLSTER

WHY: This supported bridge (Fig. 7.7) creates a stretch for your chest while releasing the front of your hips, often a problem area for runners.

HOW: Lie back onto a bolster or rolled blanket, lengthwise. Then slide your head and shoulders off the edge of the prop, so that your upper shoulders rest on the ground.

VARIATIONS: You can bend your knees, as in an active bridge pose, or stretch your legs long. They may roll to the sides; that's fine. If you'd rather keep them facing up and elevated, add another bolster below the one supporting your spine and use a strap to hold your legs together.

7.7 *Bridge on a bolster*

BRIDGE ON A BLOCK

WHY: Using a block to support your bridge pose (Fig. 7.8) provides a stronger release for your hip flexors.

HOW: Lie on your back with a yoga block in your hand, knees bent to 90 degrees, feet on the floor. Lift your hips and slide the block, set at medium height and running across your body, under the pelvis, two or three inches below your waistband. Spread your arms to the sides and relax for a minute or two.

VARIATIONS: For a more mellow bridge, use the block at its lowest height. For a stronger backbend, turn it on its short end, but be sure you trust that the block will support you, or you'll subconsciously clench instead of releasing. To help reset the sacroiliac joint, sometimes called the SI joint, rotate the block 90 degrees so its narrow edge supports the sacrum (the arrowhead-shaped bottom of the spine that inserts into the pelvis) as your ilium (the big bony bowl of the pelvis) relaxes down.

There are many choices for arm position. Relax your arms to either side for a passive chest stretch. To be more active with your chest stretch, hold the block or, if your arms are long, clasp your hands together on the far side of the block. To intensify the hip stretch, reach your arms overhead. Whatever you choose, check that your neck retains its normal curve.

If you feel steady on the block, walk your feet away from your hips (Fig. 7.9).

7.8 *Bridge on a block*

7.9 *Bridge on a block with feet apart*

Twists

These twisting poses focus on thoracic rotation. You'll work a range of motion far greater than what you need for efficient upper-body movement during the running stride, enabling you to be smooth and fluid when you run.

THREADING THE NEEDLE

WHY: This series of twists builds flexibility along the spine and ribcage, freeing room for the breath.

HOW: From hands and knees, hold your back long as you lift your left arm toward the ceiling for a few breaths (Fig. 7.10). (Don't be surprised if this is hard; most of us have tight muscles around the thoracic spine.) On an exhalation, lower your left elbow to the ground beneath your left shoulder, and take your right arm up to the ceiling as you twist in the opposite direction for a few more breaths (Fig. 7.11). Come up slowly and repeat on the second side.

VARIATIONS: If you feel stable on your elbow, try lowering all the way down to your left shoulder (Fig. 7.12). If you do this variation, be sure your neck isn't in pain.

To free more room for rotation, take your right leg off to the right of your hip, like an outrigger canoe (Fig. 7.13).

7.10 *Thoracic twist*

7.11 *Threading the needle to elbow*

7.12 *Threading the needle with shoulder lowered*

7.13 *Threading the needle with leg moved outward*

SQUAT WITH TWIST

WHY: This pose gives you the lower-leg and back stretch of the squat (see Chapter 6) while working the upper back and chest in a twist.

HOW: From a wide squat, take your right hand in front of your right foot, right triceps toward the inner right knee. Lift your left arm toward the ceiling (Fig. 7.14). After 5 to 10 breaths, repeat on the other side.

VARIATIONS: For less intensity or to really focus on the twist, push your left hand into your left knee (Fig. 7.15). For more intensity, once twisting, reach both arms wide, rotate your thumbs down, bend your elbows, and try to clasp your hands behind your back (Fig. 7.16).

7.14 *Squat with twist*

7.15 *Squat with twist, hand on knee*

7.16 *Squat with twist, hands clasped*

WIDE FORWARD FOLD WITH TWIST

WHY: This pose adds a twist to the hamstring stretch of the wide forward fold (see Chapter 4).

HOW: From a straddle, knees bent if necessary, take your left hand to the floor or a block under your face. Stretch your right arm toward the ceiling (Fig. 7.17). After 5 to 10 breaths, repeat on the other side.

VARIATIONS: For a groin stretch, let your hips angle and bend your left knee more.

To focus instead on the twist in your upper back, make a point of holding your hips level.

7.17 *Wide forward fold with twist*

PART III

FINDING
the
RIGHT
BALANCE

8

PREVENTING AND CORRECTING
OVERUSE INJURY

OVERUSE INJURIES—the injuries runners most often incur—develop as the result of an imbalance. It can be an imbalance between work and rest, when you load your body with more stress than it can recover from between your runs. But it is usually the result of an imbalance between strength and flexibility (*sthira* and *sukha*) in certain muscle groups. It can go from front to back, as in an imbalance between quadriceps strength and glute strength, or between hip flexor suppleness and hamstring strength. It can be an imbalance from left to right, with the muscles of one hip stronger or tighter than those of the other. Or it could be a top-to-bottom imbalance, when the muscles of your thighs are stronger than your lower legs, or your core is weaker than your thighs.

A well-rounded yoga program addresses these imbalances holistically, strengthening the weaker areas in your body and loosening the tighter areas. Yoga practice also gives you the time and space to pay attention to what's happening in your body, so that you can observe the state of balance or imbalance between strength and flexibility. In this chapter, we'll look at self-tests and poses to correct the most common imbalances runners incur, so that you can develop a home practice that will help you correct and prevent the fundamental causes of overuse injuries.

Balance from Front to Back: Thighs

Runners commonly identify themselves as tight through the hamstrings. This tightness can have one of two causes. It can be a consequence of short, strong hamstrings, strengthened through running. If the hamstrings get really tight, they will tug your tailbone down and lessen the curve in your lower back, which leads to discomfort as the lower back stretches too much. Sometimes, however, the hamstrings are tight because they are stretched long due to a forward tilt of the pelvis. Strength along the front of the body, through the hip flexors and quadriceps, can pull the pelvis into this anterior tilt. Such a tilt creates tightness and congestion in the lower back, and it holds the hamstrings in a lengthened position, as their attachment at the sitting bones is drawn away from their attachment at the knees. Thus they are tight from being held at the end of their stretch. Seek balance front to back, so that you won't suffer from lower-back pain.

8.1 *Low lunge*

Self-Test

Coming into a low lunge position (Fig. 8.1) will give you insight into the balance between your quadriceps and hip flexors. With your back knee down and your hands on your front knee, do you feel the stretch more in the front of the back leg (tight hip flexors), the back of the front leg (tight hamstrings), or both simultaneously? (You may also feel a stretch in the inner or outer thigh of the front leg, which is more food for thought; see "Balance from Left to Right" on page 100.)

Twisting lunge (Fig. 4.12)

Bow (Fig. 5.25)

Bridge on a block (Fig. 7.8)

additional poses

Warrior I (Fig. 4.1)
Low lunge (Fig. 4.11)
Lizard lunge (Fig. 4.13)
Reclining half Lord of the Fishes (Fig. 4.32)
Half bow (Fig. 5.26)
Reclining hero (Fig. 6.9)
Bridge on a bolster (Fig. 7.7)

Runner's lunge with ankle stretch (Fig. 4.14)

Head-to-knee (Fig. 4.28)

Downward-facing dog (Fig. 5.3)

additional poses

Standing forward fold (Fig. 4.16)
Wide forward fold, standing straddle (Fig. 4.19)
Hamstring strap stretches (Figs. 4.36–4.38)
Dolphin (Fig. 5.5)

Balance from Front to Back: Core

Higher up the kinetic chain, many runners' chest and abdominal muscles are stronger than their back muscles. If your core-strengthening routine involves a lot of crunches and little planking or back extension or if you spend a lot of your day sitting, you may have strong, short, tight muscles along the front of your core, but overstretched, relatively weak muscles along the back. Likewise, if your hamstrings are short and tight, they can pull your pelvis into that backward tilt that overstretches your back and encourages tightness in the front.

8.2 *Reverse plank*

8.3 *Boat*

Self-Test

Compare how long you can hold reverse plank with good form (Fig. 8.2) with how long you can hold boat pose with good form (Fig. 8.3). If you can hold reverse plank less than half the number of breaths as boat pose, or if reverse plank is difficult because your chest or the front of your hips are tight, focus on strengthening your back and opening your chest and hips.

Reverse table with leg lifted (Fig. 5.12)

Bird dog (Fig. 5.18)

Locust (Fig. 5.23)

Locust with arms extended (Fig. 5.24)

additional poses

Plank with opposite arm and leg lifted (Fig. 5.2)
Reverse plank (Fig. 5.10)
Reverse table (Fig. 5.11)
Cobra (Fig. 5.21)
Bridge (Fig. 5.31)

Warrior I (Fig. 4.1)

Passive backbend (Fig. 7.4)

Bridge on a bolster (Fig. 7.7)

additional poses

Pigeon backbend (Figs. 4.26–4.27)
Bow (Fig. 5.25)
Reclining hero (Fig. 6.9)
Fish on blocks (Fig. 7.6)
Bridge on a block (Fig. 7.8)

Balance from Left to Right

As we will see in Chapter 9, any single-legged standing balance pose will reveal differences between the strength and flexibility of your legs. One side may be tighter and therefore stronger; the other may be more flexible and less stable.

Endurance running, rather than running for multidirectional ball sports like soccer and lacrosse, moves you almost exclusively in the sagittal plane (front to back). Runners who don't purposefully include lateral movement can become weak along the sides of their bodies, so that the outer hips, which help stabilize in lateral motion, are underdeveloped. Combine this weakness with running on canted roads facing traffic, which drops the left hip lower than the right and stretches the outer left ankle, and you can find yourself developing a pronounced left-to-right imbalance. This can lead to hip and knee problems on one side—and these problems can reflect weakness in either hip, as pain often zigzags down the kinetic chain, expressing itself in the left hip, the right knee, and the left foot, for example.

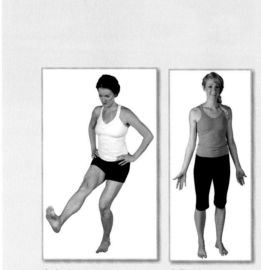

8.4 *Single-legged chair*   **8.5** *Mountain*

Self-Test

A single-legged chair pose (Fig. 8.4) can reveal tightness in the inner thigh or weakness in the outer hip. Stand in front of a mirror in mountain pose (Fig. 8.5), a steady stance. Lift your right leg out in front of you, a few inches off the ground, and take a single-legged squat with your left knee. Watch whether the knee tracks directly forward over the toes; this is the balance we are looking for. If it bows in toward the center, dropping toward the right, you'll want to focus on strengthening the outer hip and stretching the inner thigh, which happens simultaneously in the poses listed on page 101. As you repeat on the right side, notice whether one leg feels different.

Warrior II (Fig. 4.2)

Lizard lunge (Fig. 4.13)

Pigeon forward fold (Fig. 4.23)

additional poses

Warrior I (Fig. 4.1)
Exalted warrior (Fig. 4.3)
Warrior III (Fig. 4.4)
Triangle (Fig. 4.5)
Side angle (Fig. 4.6)
Pyramid (Figs. 4.7–4.8)
Cow-face (Fig. 4.21)
Reclining cow-face (Fig. 4.22)
Reclining pigeon (Fig. 4.25)
Pigeon backbend (Fig. 4.26)
Revolved head-to-knee (Fig. 4.29)
Half Lord of the Fishes (Fig. 4.30)
Lord of the Fishes (Fig. 4.31)
Reclining half Lord of the Fishes (Fig. 4.32)
Reclining twists (Figs. 4.33–4.35)

Balance from Top to Bottom

As you gain ability as a runner, you'll develop strong thighs and, hopefully, strong hips, too. There can be too much of a good thing, though, if your upper legs become disproportionately stronger than your lower legs. Your shoe choice can exacerbate this discrepancy because stability and motion-control shoes and orthotics can support the motion of the lower leg so much that the stabilizing muscles in the feet weaken.

8.4 *Single-legged chair*

Self-Test

Return to the single-legged chair pose (Fig. 8.4) in front of a mirror, observing the behavior of your lower leg. Is there visible wobbling in your lower leg? Do you roll right to left and back across the foot? (Both of these indicate relative weakness in the lower leg.) Are your toes relaxed or clenched until the knuckles are white? Circle the ankle of your lifted leg; how much range of motion do you have? As you stay, which fatigues first: your upper thigh and hip or your lower leg? If it's the lower, you'll want to focus on lower-leg strength.

Warrior III (Fig. 4.4)

Hand-to-foot, holding foot (Fig. 9.4)

Toe balance (Fig. 6.2)

additional poses

Tree (Fig. 9.1)
Eagle (Fig. 9.2)
Dancer (Fig. 9.7)

Narrow squat (Fig. 6.1)

Toe stretch (Fig. 6.10)

Half kneeling, half squat (Fig. 6.11)

additional poses

Wide squat (Fig. 6.3)
Child's pose (Fig. 6.4)
Rock (Fig. 6.6)

9

PREVENTING ACUTE INJURY

WHILE OVERUSE INJURIES are the result of an imbalance in the body, acute injuries are usually the result of an imbalance of your body in space. For those of us who love to run trails, a sense of balance in space is critical to avoiding injury, as the next sprained ankle or skinned knee is always only a step away.

Yoga's balance poses are especially good for conferring the elements of balance: strong core, hip, and lower-leg muscles; a single-pointed focus; and a good sense of proprioception, the sense of where your body is relative to the ground and obstacles.

Balance poses can be slotted through your day. Try standing in tree (Fig. 9.1) as you brush your teeth, or sinking into eagle (Fig. 9.2) after your workout. Dancer pose (Fig. 9.7), with its front-of-the-hip release, is fantastic after you've spent time in a desk chair or car seat. Provided you don't push too hard into these poses, they can stand alone without a warm-up. You'll find one or two balance poses offer a shortcut to paying attention, as they demand you focus on exactly what is happening moment to moment, breath to breath.

Single-Legged Standing Balance Poses

TREE

WHY: Tree pose (Fig. 9.1) gives you a snapshot look at your balance for the day, as well as insight into hip and core strength.

HOW: From mountain pose (Fig. 8.5), take the weight into your right leg as you point your left knee to the left and rest the left foot against the right leg. You can hold hands on hips, in prayer position, off to the sides of your shoulders, or overhead.

VARIATIONS: Your left foot can be low or high against the right leg. Low positions include resting the ball of the foot on the ground, with just the left heel resting against the right inner ankle; cupping the right calf with the arch of the left foot; or hiking the foot above the knee, which creates more of an inner-thigh stretch for the raised leg. Don't rest your foot against your right knee, though; while this seems like a good next step from the calf, the knee can do without external lateral pressure. For more challenge, close your eyes. You'll increase proprioception, your sense of where you are in space.

9.1 *Tree*

EAGLE

WHY: Eagle pose (Fig. 9.2) builds hip strength in the standing leg while stretching the wrapping leg. As a bonus, the arm position gives a fantastic stretch for your upper back.

HOW: From mountain pose (Fig. 8.5), cross your right knee tight over your left knee, bending the left knee into a single-leg squat. Cross your arms at the elbows, right under left, with the backs of the hands resting together.

VARIATIONS: For less intensity, spread your arms out like wings to help you balance.

To deepen the pose, wrap your right toes around your left calf to get a bigger stretch for the legs. Wrap your right wrist inside your left wrist and lay your palms together to get a deeper stretch for the arms.

9.2 *Eagle*

HAND-TO-FOOT

WHY: Balancing in hand-to-foot (or hand-to-knee, or strap-to-foot) strengthens your standing-leg hip and lower-leg muscles as it stretches the hamstrings of the extended leg.

HOW: Standing on your left leg, bend your right knee and hold your right shin (Fig. 9.3). Your left hand can be at your hip or off to the side.

VARIATIONS: To intensify the stretch in the raised leg, straighten the knee and hold your foot with your hand (Fig. 9.4) or a strap.

To stretch the inner thigh of the raised leg, open it to the side as you stay tall on both sides. You can turn your head and gaze away from your raised leg (Fig. 9.5).

To work your core, quadriceps, and hip flexors, stretch your raised leg straight in front of you while holding your hands to your hips or overhead for a few breaths (Fig. 9.6).

9.3 *Hand-to-foot, holding shin*

9.4 *Hand-to-foot, holding foot*

9.5 *Hand-to-foot, head turned*

9.6 *Hand-to-foot, leg extended*

DANCER

WHY: Dancer pose (Fig. 9.7) stretches the front of the hips and the chest while it engages the back muscles and the muscles of the lower leg, all critical in balance.

HOW: Standing on your left leg, bend your right knee and hold your foot in your hand. Extend your left arm overhead. Hinge from the left hip so that your chest moves forward as your right arm and leg move back.

VARIATIONS: Pause where you feel the first level of challenge. That could mean staying in the quadriceps stretch instead of doing a backbend or moving deep into the fold. Place your left hand on a wall if you feel unsteady.

A strap can help you catch the foot if your quads are very tight. It can also help you stretch your arms and deepen the backbend. With the strap around the top of the right ankle or toes, bend your elbows and hold the strap behind your head with both hands (Fig. 9.8).

9.7 *Dancer*

9.8 *Dancer with strap*

Arm Balancing

Beyond finding balance on your feet, it's useful to practice standing on your hands. Playing with arm balance poses gives you an opportunity to find new ways to control your body in space, and it sets up a relatively safe, controlled environment in which you can fall. Knowing what goes into a fall and how to land are important lessons in coping with and preventing future falls.

If your fear of falling is great, pad your practice area with blankets or towels. Be sure also to maintain a sense of humor and play as you experiment with arm balances. Sometimes lightening up makes you feel lighter and float higher.

The arm balance poses both require and build healthy wrists, elbows, and shoulders, and they also develop strength in your upper body, which is useful should you need to catch yourself in case of a fall while running. If you are already injured, be sure not to irritate already inflamed shoulders, elbows, or wrists by stubbornly practicing too many arm balances.

CRANE (a.k.a. CROW)

WHY: This arm balance activates your core muscles, teaches you about balancing in space, and gives you a low height from which to practice falling.

HOW: Come into a wide squat and lift to your tiptoes. Set your hands on the floor under your shoulders, bending elbows back as for *chaturanga* (Fig. 5.6). Place the inside of your knees on your triceps and try lifting one or both feet up as you balance on your hands (Fig. 9.9).

VARIATIONS: Tight runners' hips can limit you from getting your knees high on your upper arms. Standing on a block can assist with placing your shins on your triceps.

If you're afraid of falling, create a soft landing by stacking blankets or pillows in front of you. You can even lower your head to the cushion to see how it feels to lean all your weight forward.

9.9 Crane

SHOULDER-PRESSURE POSE

WHY: Shoulder-pressure pose teaches you to shift your weight into your arms and lift from your core. A fall from here is no less harmful than sliding down a very short fire pole.

HOW: From a wide squat, work your elbows under your thighs and rest with your hands a little more than shoulder width apart (Fig. 9.10). Wiggle your big toes close together as you bend your elbows, keeping them close to your sides. Try squeezing your knees toward each other to lift your feet and cross at the ankles (Fig. 9.11).

VARIATIONS: For more challenge, work your arms toward straight. For even more challenge, unhook your ankles and spread your legs into a straddle for firefly (Fig. 9.12).

9.10 *Shoulder-pressure*

9.11 *Shoulder-pressure, ankles crossed*

9.12 *Firefly*

10

BALANCING WORK AND REST

IF YOU WANT your running to improve, you need both consistency and variety. You must run consistently first, establishing an aerobic base, acclimating your soft tissues to the demands of mileage, and creating a mental routine to support your training. Then, to reach the next level, you need to introduce variety—harder runs, easier runs, runs over changing terrain, longer runs, runs at various paces.

This balance must also appear in the amount of work you do and the amount of rest you do. You can't pile on the miles and intensity without burning out, and you can't rest too much without losing fitness. Finding the right balance of work and rest in your training is critical to your success and your longevity as a runner, and yoga can help.

Yoga and the Work/Rest Balance

Yoga can constitute work, or it can count as rest. The style, intensity, and frequency with which you practice will determine whether you are adding training stress or enjoying recovery. Since "doing yoga" can mean anything from dropping from handstand to *chaturanga* to moving deep into a hamstring stretch to resting in supported child's pose or sitting in meditation, you'll need to consider the yoga that will best help you find the work/rest balance in your training.

Tracking Work and Rest

Add your yoga practice to your training log, with notes about the intensity of the practice and comments about what was included and how it went. Track it on the same page as the workouts themselves, so that you can ensure you have peaks of work and valleys of rest, instead of a constant influx of stress on your body.

Your off-season and base-building periods, when you are running consistently easy, are the time for a more physically rigorous yoga practice. If you were to pick up the same practice later in the season, it might well be too intense for you. That's why I suggest trying new, vigorous forms of yoga well away from competition—so that you don't overtax your muscles or tendons and so that you are able to conserve your energy to use when it matters most for your running.

As you begin to focus your training toward a season or event, you'll need to tone down your yoga practice. Two or three trips a week to the studio for a power flow class can become once-weekly visits. This will maintain the gains you make in the base period while still helping you strike the right work/rest balance.

Closer to the peak event on your schedule, you'll need to lighten your practice even more. One ill-advised move in a sweaty, energy-packed group class can ruin your race. Look for gentle and restorative classes or take a break from the studio in favor of a softer home practice.

Restorative yoga can be an important part of your recovery strategy. In restorative poses, you give your nervous system a break from the action of training and the stressors of daily life, offering yourself the opportunity to relax, rejuvenate, and restore on a deep cellular level. For more on this practice, see Chapter 18.

Yoga's Psychological Approach

Beyond the physical, yoga can help with the work/rest balance by giving you the psychological tools to know when to rest—and when to push.

TAPPING INTO YOUR STRENGTH

Group practice, especially with an inspiring teacher or an energetic group, can teach you ways to tap into your strength, finding reserves you may not have realized were there. Attempting a new move, such as a lift into headstand or a jump from crow pose to *chaturanga*, can shore up your sense of playfulness while revealing that you are able to do much, much more than you may expect. You may find yourself staying in a strength pose like chair for what feels like forty breaths as the teacher gives adjustments and lectures. These are opportunities to test the limits of your ability to push. Often, you find that you can push harder than you thought. As you practice this in class, you'll develop a useful tool for hanging on to hard run paces.

Similarly, being deep in a still pose, as in yin yoga, and remaining passive even as the intensity grows teaches you how to relax in the face of intensity. Moving through slow-paced breath exercises while staying loose, even as you want to gasp for air, will show you ways to manage your compulsion to stop and instead to keep going. These opportunities test the limits of your ability to endure. Often, you find that you can endure longer than you thought, which gives you the confidence to push over longer distances.

ACCEPTING RELEASE

Yoga also teaches you how to grow efficient in your movements, to dial back the amount of muscular engagement you bring to poses and the mental effort you bring to situations. Over time, we learn to surrender the need to control everything all the time. When you are on the mat, investigate where you are doing more than necessary. Are you grasping with your standing foot in one-legged balance poses? Are your glutes overengaged in backbends? When you are on the road or trail, notice where you are holding tension. Do your shoulders hike up? Are your fists clenched? When you are dealing with yourself and others, in work, family, and relationships, are you spending your energy wisely? Or are you doing more than you need to for no reward?

"THE WISDOM TO KNOW THE DIFFERENCE"

Practicing yoga and mindfulness will help you discern what you can change and what you can't in your body and in your life. To paraphrase Reinhold Niebuhr's serenity prayer, it gives you the serenity to accept the things you cannot change, the courage to change the things you can, and the wisdom to know the difference.

When you learn to listen to your body and your intuitive mind, you'll be able to read the signals from your muscles, joints, and mood. When you feel sore, creaky,

In and out of Your Control

As you plan your next race (or work project, or family trip), make a list of issues that cause you anxiety. Then note each one as "in my control" or "out of my control." For the items that are in your control, note the first few action steps to resolve the issue. For the items that are out of your control, plan to shift your attitude about the issue, lest you cause yourself suffering.

and cranky, take preemptive rest to help restore the work/rest balance. When you feel strong, fluid, and happy, consider whether you might safely push a little more. The implications for your sport and your life are priceless. You'll learn to distinguish the right time to work from the right time to rest.

Recovery Matters

Rest is critical to your training and success as a runner and as a person. It is during rest and recovery that your body adapts to the work of your training and the stressors of your life, so you must ensure your rest and recovery are adequate relative to the strain of your running, your yoga practice, and your duties.

As mentioned, at certain points in your training cycle, a moderate-to-mellow yoga practice will aid your recovery; at other points, even that can be too intense. While restorative yoga is always a fine choice, there will be days and even weeks when you are better served staying at home with a pillow than dragging yourself to the studio for a class that is too intense for your body's needs. Don't hesitate to listen to your intuition. Not everything is a test of your will to push. Often, you gain more by doing much, much less.

For a complete explanation of the role recovery and restorative yoga play in your training, please read my book *The Athlete's Guide to Recovery.*

11

BALANCING STUDIO YOGA
WITH HOME PRACTICE

I RAN WITH a friend who was deep in heavy training, seven weeks before she raced Ironman Lake Placid. She told me she'd come to my studio for a class with one of our most popular teachers, and while it was a lovely practice, "It was too hard for me right now." I was heartened to hear her admit that. The needs of an athlete in training are very different from the needs of many yoga students. While a sweaty flow yoga class can be a fantastic workout, there are big portions of the training cycle where it can be too much work for a serious runner. And just because you *can* do most or all of a hard class doesn't mean that you should. Pushing too hard on the mat can undermine the work you've been doing in your training. It comes back to intention: Why are you doing your yoga practice? Is it complementing your training? Or is it a forum for competition?

This is why home practice is especially useful for athletes. At home, you can focus on exactly what you need to be doing, moving at your own pace, staying in each pose for as long or as short a stay as suits you.

At the same time, though, it's useful to visit classes regularly. Classes will push you in different ways. The teacher will keep her eye on you, ensuring that you aren't developing bad alignment habits that could put you at risk of injury. Class is where you learn new things, refreshing your vocabulary of poses. You'll be encouraged to approach poses, sequences, and techniques differently than you would at home. Making a wise decision about which class to take and how to practice in class will ensure you receive the benefits of group practice without undermining your training.

How to Choose a Class

Yoga studio schedules can be overwhelming. Some use Sanskrit words, while others deploy various English names to describe classes. Some use levels, while others don't. If you're flummoxed by a schedule, your best bet is to call the studio and speak to the owner about what would work for you. (I'm always happy to take these calls at my studio. The answers to a few questions, such as where they are in their training, whether they like minimal or explicit instruction, and how they feel about crowds, let me make recommendations, saving them the process of trial-and-error in finding the right class and teacher.)

See Table 11.1 for a list of yoga styles and their best uses for athletes. The following sections explain terms you'll commonly see on studio schedules.

TABLE 11.1 YOGA STYLES

Style	Good for . . .	In the . . .
Anusara	Refining alignment, backbends	Base and build periods
Ashtanga	Building strength	Base period
Bikram/Barkan/hot	Flexibility and focus	Base period
Hatha	Beginners	Base, build, and peak periods
Iyengar	Refining alignment, beginners	Base and build periods
Kripalu	Flexibility, self-awareness	Base and build periods
Pilates/Yogalates/Core Fusion	Core strength	Base and build periods
Restorative	Recovery	Base, build, and especially peak periods
Vinyasa/Flow/Power	Building strength	Base period

1–2 (or 1/2), 2–3 (or 2/3), 1–3

These denote levels, where level 1 is beginner, level 2 is intermediate, and level 3 is advanced. An advanced practitioner can have a profound experience in a basic class, and a beginner can enjoy an advanced class with the right attitude and instruction. Use these numbers to help you decode how complicated the asana practice is going to be.

GOOD FOR: helping you determine whether a class will be more or less demanding, which is critical when you require practices that will not wear you out during peak running periods.

HATHA

Hatha refers to the physical practice of the poses and to their work connecting the sun (*ha*) and moon (*tha*) energies in the body. In the West, though, *hatha* is used to describe a slow-paced class in which poses are held for extended periods. These poses and classes are usually quite gentle, depending on the instructor.

GOOD FOR: getting to know how your body feels in each pose. Take these classes at any point in the training cycle, except the few days immediately before or after a long race.

VINYASA, FLOW, POWER

These terms, either separate or in conjunction, denote a faster-paced style in which practitioners move from pose to pose with the breath. Because of the movement, there is typically less emphasis on alignment, so it's helpful to have a sense of proper alignment before attending a flow class (this book will help, as will a few basic classes). Rooms may be heated to 80 or 90 degrees, so be careful about when in your training cycle and how often you practice, lest you pile on too much intensity.

Many styles affiliated with nationally recognized teachers—Baptiste Power Yoga, Shiva Rea's Prana Flow Yoga, David Life and Sharon Gannon's Jivamukti Yoga, or Ana Forrest's Forrest Yoga—are variations on *vinyasa* yoga.

GOOD FOR: building strength during your off-season and base periods. For experienced runner-yogis, one or two weekly classes during the build period can help maintain strength gains from the base period. Drop any rigorous flow classes by the week of your peak race.

ASHTANGA, MYSORE

A quick-moving sequence of poses, Ashtanga's Primary Series focuses on forward folds interlaced with a standard *vinyasa*, or flow, of *chaturanga*, upward-facing dog, and downward-facing dog. It is taught either in classes led by yoga instructors or in "Mysore style," named after the city in India where the style's founder, K. Pattabhi Jois, taught until his death in 2009. In this approach, students move through the sequence at their own pace and receive individual instruction from the teacher.

GOOD FOR: building strength during your off-season and base periods. For experienced runner-yogis, one or two weekly classes during the build period can help maintain strength gains from the base period. Ashtanga places special emphasis on breathing and moving energy in the body using *bandhas,* or "locks," which can help runners build body awareness and focus.

IYENGAR

The Iyengar approach, named for B. K. S. Iyengar, author of *Light on Yoga,* emphasizes precise alignment, often with the use of props. Classes move slowly, with a focus on getting each pose right rather than moving quickly. Certified Iyengar teachers are rigorously trained and can usually provide a wealth of anatomical information.

GOOD FOR: inquisitive minds; learning the fundamentals of the poses. Runners can build strength, flexibility, and focus in Iyengar classes. As with generic *hatha* yoga classes, an Iyengar class can fit anywhere in the cycle apart from the few days before and after a peak race.

ANUSARA

Like Iyengar Yoga, Anusara pays attention to alignment, using a language of loops and spirals to describe the poses. A friendly, playful style, Anusara offers plenty of backbends ("heart opening"). Classes are often run in series, which allows each week's lesson to build on the preceding one.

GOOD FOR: back strength and chest openness; sense of humor. Runners new to yoga would be well served to sign up for a level 1 Anusara series to learn the basics of the poses with a teacher's eye on them. As with other *hatha* yoga classes, Anusara classes can fit into most parts of the training cycle, but not too close to a race.

KRIPALU

Kripalu Yoga is affiliated with the Kripalu Center for Yoga and Health, a retreat center in the Berkshires of western Massachusetts. The Kripalu style emphasizes the student's experience, setting up a structure wherein each student can investigate different expressions of the poses, determining what works for them. This freedom is nice for athletes in a class: They have the opportunity to do less or more, given how their bodies are reacting on a given day.

GOOD FOR: self-expression. Gentle classes are appropriate year-round; moderate classes will work best in your build period; and vigorous classes can be added in the off-season or for strength maintenance in the base and build periods.

RESTORATIVE

Restorative yoga uses a host of soft props—blankets, bolsters, eye pillows—to support the body in various relaxing poses. The goal is not to stretch but rather to enforce downtime in soothing positions. Staying in these padded poses helps balance your nervous system, engaging the parasympathetic side of it and aiding athletic recovery.

GOOD FOR: recovery from long and hard workouts; rest before and after a peak event. If you have access to restorative classes or private lessons, treat yourself. Having an experienced teacher settle you into the poses can lead to even more release than doing them yourself, as I outline in Part V. A restorative yoga class is a perfect rest-day, taper week, or post-race activity.

BIKRAM, BARKAN

These branded styles of hot yoga follow a set sequence of poses in a room heated to over 100 degrees. Jimmy Barkan, a senior teacher under Bikram Choudhury, founder of Bikram Yoga, developed his own style, which is similar to Bikram but with slightly more variety in the pose sequence. See the sidebar on page 123 for more on hot yoga.

GOOD FOR: the off-season, especially in cold climates. Runners must take care not to push too hard. The language of a Bikram Yoga class includes exhortations to "push beyond your flexibility" and to "lock your knees." Please don't do either. Stay within your limits, be sure you aren't lapsing into the mindset of being in a gymnastics competition, and take what works for you.

PILATES, YOGALATES, AND CORE FUSION

While they are not technically yoga, these core-focused classes can be found at many yoga studios, often taught by yoga instructors. Depending on the teacher, they can include a mind-body-breath component or can feel more like exercise classes. Regardless, the focus on your core muscles will have a direct positive effect on your running, provided you practice carefully and don't do too much too close to a peak race.

GOOD FOR: building and maintaining core strength in the base and build periods. Core strength, of course, helps prevent injuries.

Scheduling Your Class

Now that you know how to read the studio schedule, you can go about choosing a class that fits with your training plan. You'll want to make sure that the intensity of the practice and the intensity of your workouts don't combine to put more stress on your body than you can handle. You'll have to experiment to find the right mix.

Remember to periodize your yoga practice in inverse proportion to your training. If you are in an easy, base-building period of your training cycle, you'll have the energy to build strength in a *vinyasa* style of yoga. As your running intensifies, you might pull back and choose a gentler approach or cut down the number of flow practices you do weekly. And as you approach your peak, stick to very gentle or restorative classes.

What to Look for in a Teacher

Just as one need not be a sub-4:00 miler to coach track well, one need not be a runner to teach a great yoga class for athletes. However, if you can find a teacher who has a sports background, all the better. As we've seen, the effects of running on your body often run completely counter to the effects of a physical yoga practice. A teacher who does not run may or may not empathize with a runner's tightnesses, strengths, and weaknesses. A teacher who runs will understand innately the needs of athletes in class.

In particular, a teacher who is familiar with the principles of periodization and the demands of high mileage on an athlete's body will offer a more sympathetic approach to practice. Yoga teachers are, by nature, sympathetic folks, though, so don't hesitate to study with anyone whose style speaks to you. Just be careful if you find yourself attracted to drill-sergeant-style instructors who encourage you to go, to push, to constantly work at your edge. While it feels like it's productive, this style of practice

Heated Rooms

Many studios offer hot yoga, or warm yoga, in a room that's heated to temperatures ranging from 80 to 105 degrees. While the external heat can warm you up faster and allow you to move toward the extreme edges of your flexibility, that's not a good thing for a serious runner in the midst of a training cycle. For one, many athletes already spend their days in a state of semidehydration; practicing in a room designed to make you sweat more will only exacerbate this issue. When you feel flexible because of the heat, you're more likely to stretch too much, especially when the teacher's language encourages you to push.

✦ *Before you practice hot yoga, consider where you are in your training. If it's your off-season and you can take care not to overstretch, go for it. In season, be wary of adding too much training stress and putting your body in a position where you might overstretch.*

may be directly at odds with your training goals. Remember: Your yoga practice is meant to complement your training, not be an extension of it.

Finding the right teacher is a little like finding the right running shoe. Some folks need more support and look for a stabilizing shoe; the yoga analogy would be a teacher who spends a lot of time on alignment and corrections. Others do fine in lightweight trainers, flats, or spikes; here, the analogy would be a teacher who simply calls out the names of the poses, providing a minimal structure to class without controlling the students' precise motions.

On a bigger level, teachers subscribe to various styles and approaches to yoga. To keep with the running shoe metaphor, some athletes sample a range of brands and rotate among them over the course of a week. Others find one that works for them and never deviate. Just as one brand of shoe might not feel right to you, one style of yoga or teacher may not resonate for you. Shoe brands will tweak their models from year to year, and you might find that the shoes that worked so well for you have now changed to the point where they don't feel right. Similarly, teachers change as they learn and grow; you might find one teacher's approach isn't working for your needs in the moment but may in the future.

How to Practice in Class

Take a moment or two before class to center yourself and to affirm your intention for practice. If you are far from a peak run, remind yourself that it's OK to push, OK to fall out of balance poses, OK to stay a few breaths longer than you think you can. If you are close to a hard workout or race, however, you should consider the opposite: It's OK to rest; it's OK to take child's pose; it's OK to choose the easier variation of a tough pose. Then follow through on your commitment to yourself. Keep returning to this intention: Is this a time to push or a time to rest?

Talking to your teacher about your training goals and the state of your body will help, as well. Make sure the teacher knows when you are planning on taking it easy. Apprise him or her of any injuries or tweaks you're feeling, so that he or she won't adjust you in ways that would exacerbate these issues. A well-intentioned but too-forceful touch can cause a tear in the hamstring attachment or a strain on the rotator cuff muscles. Don't be afraid to communicate with your teacher about what feels good and what feels dangerous.

Surround yourself with a host of props. You'll be more likely to use them if they are at hand. Blocks and straps can help you achieve poses that would otherwise be inaccessible. There is no shame in using props. Think of them not as a crutch but as a tool toward greater comfort and ability. In time, you may not need them. Alternatively, try using props when you usually don't, and you might find a happy sense of freedom and a new approach to a pose.

Designing Your Home Practice

This book is designed to help you establish a strong home yoga practice. The poses outlined in Part II and the routines you'll find in Part V will constitute this practice, which can happen before, during, and after your runs, as well as in stand-alone sessions. Deciding on poses and routines will help you overcome one of the biggest hurdles to establishing a home practice. When you begin, it's useful to have a list of things you plan to do. As you become more comfortable with home practice, you can develop a more spontaneous approach. You might start with a few poses in mind but deviate from your plan, going where your body, breath, and intuition take you. But at first, use the material in this book to give you a jumping-off point.

The other big hurdle to home practice is making the time and the space to practice. Space in your home away from distractions, particularly electronics, children, and animals, is critical. So is making the time for the practice to evolve. This might mean getting up early or watching one fewer TV show in the evening. But just as you find ways to get your run in when it really matters, your home practice will happen if you set aside a time and place for it.

Video Classes

Somewhere in between studio classes and home practice lies the terrain of video classes, either on DVDs, downloaded to your computer or mobile device, or streamed online from sites like YogaVibes (yogavibes.com). Some DVDs, like my *Athlete's Guide to Yoga: A Personalized Practice,* allow you to pick and choose among the various segments to create a customized routine.

Video classes combine the energy of a led practice with the convenience of being at home and on your own time. They are especially useful as you make the transition to doing yoga outside the studio because they give you ideas and instruction while allowing you to hit *pause* if you'd like to stay in a pose for a long time or *rewind* if you need to repeat.

One benefit of streaming classes online is the range of fresh content available online. You can try classes by different teachers, especially if you might like to travel to study with one of them in person. Or you can stick with one teacher, learning his or her approach to different sequences. My weekly "Yoga for Athletes" classes, for example, appear at YogaVibes. You'll see some of the poses and sequences from this book there, but they appear in different combinations and with different emphases and insights each week.

The very thing that makes video classes a hybrid of studio and home practice, however, is also their shadow side. You don't get the benefit of having the instructor's eyes and hands on you, and your form may get sloppy. And since you are following a prerecorded practice, you won't be developing the skill of choosing the poses that work for you day to day. Use video classes as a healthy piece of your practice, but don't rely on them exclusively.

SPACE

The space for your home practice does not need to be big. You simply need a place for a sticky mat and room for your arms to spread on either side of it. A guest room might be a good place, as it tends to be relatively free of distractions, electronics, and associations. If you use a more heavily trafficked location in your home, turn your mat so it's facing in an unfamiliar direction. Face the wall, for example, rather than the television.

If you have room, keep your props and mat set up, so that you can simply drop in to your dedicated yoga space. If you need to break down your yoga space to use the room for something else, you can make the reestablishment of the space into a ritual.

Unroll your mat and align it. Set up props in neat stacks. This process of *saucha*, or "cleanliness," makes the space feel pure and special.

TIME

If you plan workouts ahead of time, whether in a paper log, spreadsheet, or online training calendar, include your home yoga practice as part of the schedule. When you're done, log it as you would a run or strength session. Watching the minutes add up will help keep you consistent.

You don't need to have long sessions each day to have a healthy home practice. Ten or 15 minutes most days of the week, with one or two longer sessions of half an hour to an hour, will do nicely. If you find yourself routinely cutting sessions short, whether out of boredom or a feeling that there's something else more important you should be doing, set a timer. It's normal to get distracted. You probably experience the same feelings on a run, but when you're running, you are covering ground. Unless you're at the track, it can be quite a ways back to your starting point, and the sheer distance is often enough impetus to keep you going. On the mat, though, putting a premature end to the session is always just a step or two away. Enduring the periods where you feel compelled to quit is an important part of your practice, one with direct positive effects for your running and for your presence in your relationships and your life.

Striking a Balance Between Home and Studio

Both studio classes and home practice serve a valuable role. You'll need to learn to strike the right balance between them. If you're too reliant on your instructors to lead you through practice, you're not developing your powers of intuition and honing your mind-body awareness, thereby missing out on an important aid for your running. If you practice exclusively at home, you become a closed circuit, unable to draw energy and inspiration from others.

You probably naturally trend toward one side or the other of this ratio, preferring to join a group or go it alone. (This is probably also echoed in your choices about running with a group or solo.) Notice which you choose, and make a conscious effort to include some of the other approach. If you are a studio junkie, try slotting just three 10-minute sessions in at home each week. If you are a home-practice aficionado, choose a class or workshop each month or so to bring freshness to your usual home routines.

PART IV

EXERCISES
for
FOCUS

12

YOGA'S EIGHT-LIMBED APPROACH

JUST AS STRENGTH and flexibility, *sthira* and *sukha,* are intimately tied, focus is a base note that threads through the physical practice. It can be sharpened in several ways: in breath exercises, in meditation, and in training. A focused runner is more competitive, especially in tough races. In this part, we'll look at yoga's benefits beyond the physical, beginning with an investigation of yoga philosophy as outlined in the *Yoga Sutras.*

These *sutras,* or aphorisms, are a short, terse collection of advice on how yoga, or union, is achieved. If you are interested in yoga philosophy, you can explore them in depth with an experienced teacher and through a personal study of various translations, which run the gamut from oblique to accessible. Some of the classic translations include versions by Swami Satchidananda and B. K. S. Iyengar, and the more accessible version by T. K. V. Desikachar in *The Heart of Yoga.* Contemporary translations such as that by Geshe Michael Roach and the recent one by Nischala Joy Devi seek to make the sutras more accessible to a modern audience.

The *Yoga Sutras* are the seminal yoga text; in this chapter, we'll look at how they have special application to runners. Other texts carry definitions of yoga that will ring familiar to the runner. For example, the *Bhagavad Gita,* a much more discursive explanation of yoga philosophy, emphasizes yoga as action (karma yoga), valuing work with a nonattachment to the fruits of our labors as the key to happiness. Runners who cleave to their training schedules can appreciate this disciplined approach. I hope you will continue to read about and study the philosophical approach laid out in both ancient and modern texts because such inquiry will deepen your understanding of your experience in running and in life.

Yama

The sutras describe the eight limbs on the path to achieving yoga, or union. The first four steps have to do with how you move through the world. First among them are the *yamas*, or restraints, which detail behaviors to avoid to remove the causes of suffering. When we live according to these principles, we lessen the effects of these negative behaviors on ourselves and those around us. The five restraints are not harming (*ahimsa*), being truthful (*satya*), not stealing (*asteya*), not grasping (*aparigraha*), and not wasting our energy (*brahmacharya*).

Each of these *yamas* has a direct application to typical runners' behavior. The first one, not harming, seems an easy one to abide by in your running life, until you consider how often runners ignore the symptoms of overuse injuries and continue training until the injury becomes severe. Denial about pain in your shin, for example, can eventually lead to a tibial stress fracture. Practicing the second restraint, *satya*, encourages honesty about what is going on in your body. In combination with not harming, it can save you from the injuries that plague many runners and frustrate your running. Practicing honesty also helps you set reasonable running goals. Knowing the true state of your current fitness helps you pace yourself correctly, which is especially important in longer races. A dishonest sense of your abilities can encourage you to start far too fast in a race or to deny yourself a peak performance by starting too slowly.

{ *exercise* }

Practice honesty about what you feel in your body, remembering that you should avoid harming yourself and others. When you do pull back when you might have pushed, be pleased and have faith that it is the right decision.

The principles of not stealing (*asteya*) and not grasping (*aparigraha*) go together. Don't steal from yourself by underestimating your talent, but don't overreach and cause yourself suffering you might have avoided. In your relationship with other runners, as well, you should not cheat on the course or indulge in envy or jealousy. The negative behaviors of stealing and coveting both come from an inherent sense of scarcity. When you steal, you are operating from a fear that there is not enough. When you envy others, you are operating from that same fear—that there aren't enough spots on the team or age-group awards or speed or talent to go around. Yoga helps you gain confidence in your own abundant strength, and when you tune in to your own inherent ability, you won't feel compelled to cheat or covet.

{ exercise }

Notice the internal dialogue that arises when you compare yourself to others. Does it reveal a sense of scarcity or lack? Can you instead consider your strengths?

Finally, the practice of *brahmacharya* teaches appropriate use of energy. In classical interpretations, the term refers to sexual chastity. In modern applications, especially for runners, it directs us to consider the very best use of our physical energy, to direct it in the appropriate pathways, and to relax everywhere else we can. This practice directly enhances your endurance, efficiency, and self-control. As you run, at every pace, consider: *Am I using the right amount of energy for my goals now? Could I relax more?* Running and moving through your day, continually returning to the most efficient form for the task at hand, are good laboratories for *brahmacharya*.

{ exercise }

As you run, try to use only the energy you need to complete what you are doing. Look for places to relax, both in your body and in your mind. Observe whether freeing up your resources in this way improves your overall running experience.

Niyama

The next step toward yoga is *niyama*. In *niyama*, we practice observances that increase our sense of happiness: cleanliness (*saucha*), contentment (*santosha*), discipline *(tapas)*, self-study (*svadyaya*), and surrender (*ishvara pranidhana*).

Running can get messy, obviously, and the goal of *saucha* is not remaining fresh as a daisy but staying pure in your focus. To that end, physical cleanliness in the form of a healthy diet and a well-organized living space and life will support your disciplined work toward your goals. When our running gear is organized and our training plans are neatly laid out, we are more likely to direct our energy toward our goals in appropriate ways. *Saucha* also covers choosing the foods, training partners, and friends that support our clear pursuit of our goals instead of muddying our path.

{ *exercise* }

Take time to arrange your running gear neatly, and see how that affects your attitude. Organize your training plan and your log. Having an orderly approach to running can free up energy for better effort in your workouts.

The right attitude can make or break your yoga practice session, workout, race, and season. Practicing *santosha*, or contentment, will allow you to reduce the suffering and increase the happiness in your daily life. Shifting your attitude, of course, is tougher than simply telling yourself, "Buck up!" It's a work in constant progress. Start small by practicing contentment with positive elements of your day: Take the time to appreciate the beautiful weather, or be appreciative of your training partner or your meal, or of having the strength and health to push yourself in a run or on the mat. The more you can cultivate a relaxed sense of happiness with the mundane elements of your life, the more you'll be able to develop equanimity. Equanimity gives you the balance to stay centered whether things are going well or not. Be happy with what is at every opportunity, and you'll find ways to stay steady even when things aren't going your way. Practicing contentment will help you enjoy even runs that aren't paced as you'd hoped, runs when you bonk, runs when you fall, and runs when you're outdone by all your training partners. Find contentment in your ability to run at all.

{ *exercise* }

During a run or meditation, reflect on a favorite running moment. Next, contemplate a positive experience from the last week of running. Finally, choose a moment from your last workout when you found joy: watching the sunrise, making your split times, or simply feeling good enough to head out the door.

Tapas refers to the discipline and zeal that push you to create change. This effort is familiar to most runners. It's the drive that pulls us through yet another interval repeat, that pushes us through the rough spots of the marathon, that keeps us going when the urge to stop is almost overwhelming. *Tapas* pushes us to change the things that we can.

In order to know what we can change, we need *svadyaya*, or self-knowledge. This comes through continued inquiry, in running, on the mat, in our daily lives. We watch how we react when things get intense. We learn tools to increase our focus. We begin to discover what we are made of by putting ourselves into situations that challenge us, be it mile repeats, balance poses, or public speaking. Along the way, we gain awareness of what elements of our nature and the world around us we can control and how to marshal our energies to deploy them where they can create change, instead of wasting our efforts on things we can't change.

The last *niyama*, *ishvara pranidhana*, asks for surrender. When we find things in life, in yoga, and in running that we cannot change through our effort, the best choice is to surrender to them. Through surrender, we use our energy most efficiently—instead of railing against circumstances that are beyond our control, we give in. The better we are able to surrender to things we can't change, the more energy we retain to create change in areas where we do have control.

{ exercise }

As you prepare for your next goal race, notice the thoughts that arise concerning the race. Are your concerns inside or outside your control? If you can control them, note how; if you cannot, choose a mantra (for example, "Oh, well") to repeat if the issues manifest on race day.

Asana

The physical poses of yoga—asanas—comprise the third limb. The *Yoga Sutras* say nothing about asana other than that it should be steady and easy, reflecting strength and flexibility. Yet asana constitutes the bulk of yoga practice in the twenty-first-century West. Most of the poses we practice are relatively recent inventions, related as much to gymnastics and calisthenics as to classical yoga practices. The goal of the physical practice is to build the strength and flexibility for a steady seat so that the practitioner can focus on the next limbs of yoga without an aching back and tight hips as a distraction.

As a runner, your goal is probably similar: developing a strong spine and flexible hips so that you can move with more freedom in your run, focusing not on aches or tightness but on the connection running fosters between body, breath, and mind. To that end, on the run and on the mat, come back to the most stable and easy form you can muster. This will help you find and maintain efficiency, freeing your energy to go longer and to pay attention to what is happening moment to moment.

Pranayama

The fourth limb involves your breath and the life force it embodies, *prana*. As we saw above, *yama* means restraint. Depending on the interpretation, *pranayama* can refer to the restraint and control of the breath in breath exercises. In an alternative reading, it concerns the removal of any restraint on the free flow of the life force. In line with this second interpretation, I think of *pranayama* as using the correct breath for the task at hand.

Depending on your goals, that breath could look very different. If you're trying to develop awareness of the breath so that you can control it in different circumstances, breath exercises like those described in the next chapter are very useful. If you're running at an easy pace, a different breath will be in order, one that's free, organic, and allows you to carry on a conversation with your training partners. If you're running a tempo pace, you'll need a different, more rhythmic breath, and if you're running a quarter-mile race, the right breath to feed that effort will be different still.

Similarly, the correct breath to support your yoga postures varies according to the posture. It could be a strong breath in a plank pose, or a relaxed, easy breath in corpse pose. Come into the best form for the task at hand, whether it's holding a pose or running, and then look for the breath that suits the shape you're taking.

{ *exercise* }

Choose a moment in your day to notice how your breath is moving. Is it appropriate for what you are doing? Ask yourself this question through the day: in traffic, during warm-up, in hard intervals, at dinner, at rest. See where you can relax a little more.

Pratyahara

The final four limbs of yoga's eight-limbed approach focus on internal experience, beginning with *pratyahara*, or sensory withdrawal, which means turning awareness to what is happening inside. When you are comfortable paying attention to what is happening inside your body and able to drown out external distractions, you'll be able to focus on the connections established in the three final limbs.

The skill of listening to your body is especially valuable for pacing your run, and thus for endurance. We practice it on the mat, as we direct our awareness away from other students in the room, away from electronic distractions at home, and back to the most efficient form we can find and to the breath that serves the needs of the pose or exercise.

A useful tool for engaging in *pratyahara* is to notice the data coming in through your senses, then to soften your awareness. For example, notice the sights around you and then soften your awareness of them, using only as much as you need to maintain what you're doing. If you're running, for example, you'll need to watch your step; if you're practicing yoga, close your eyes or soften your gaze so that you can withdraw from engagement in what's happening around you. Do the same with the sense of hearing, listening for sounds, then listening to sounds closer and closer to your body. Tune out the crowd around you in a race; tune in to the sound of your footfalls. Tune out the music in yoga class or the sound of your family members outside the room; tune in to your own breath.

In this way, *pratyahara* is a reverse of Timothy Leary's famous countercultural directive, "Turn on, tune in, drop out." You'll turn *off* the noise from the outside world (including any music you're used to running with), tune *up* your form by feeling where you might be using too much energy, and drop *in* to the sensations present on the inside. As you learn to pay attention to the sensations of intensity brought by your running and asana and meditation practices, you'll be able to explore them and to watch them shift. Comfort with the discomfort of intensity is key to success in running, in yoga, and in life.

{ *exercise* }

**Over the course of your day and your workout,
take time out to consider what is going on inside.
Tune out sights and sounds and tune in to the internal
experience. What is happening within in this moment?**

Dharana

Once you've learned to draw your attention away from the outside world and into interior space, you'll be able to practice the sixth limb, *dharana*. This is single-pointed concentration, focusing all your awareness on one thing. That thing could be a visual point, the focus called *drishti* (gazing point). You'll find this useful in running when you look at a competitor just in front of you, at the space in front of your feet, at the horizon, or at the finish-line banner. In each of these cases, *dharana* is intense concentration of your gaze, *drishti*, on that item. On the mat, your gazing point can create focus in a balance pose, acting almost as an extra limb to help you stabilize in an arm-balancing pose or to tether you to the wall in a standing balance pose.

Verbally, a mantra will help you with *dharana* by providing you with a singular item on which to focus your mind. This mantra could be as short as a syllable or as long as a phrase or chain of words. As you internally repeat the mantra, the meaning of the words grows less important and yields to the state of *dharana* created through the repetition. You'll find details on how to use mantras and *drishti* during a run in Chapter 16.

{ *exercise* }

**Choose a word on this page and give it your sole focus
for the next 10 breaths. Next time you are in line at the
grocery store, choose an item and give it your full attention
for 10 breaths. On each run, choose a mantra to focus on
for 10 or more breaths at a time.**

Diyana

Once you have developed the capacity for concentrating on one thing well, you'll be able to hold your consciousness on many things at once. This meditative state is called *diyana*. It can also be called flow. Psychologist Mihály Csíkszentmihályi describes flow in terms of the challenge of the task at hand and the proficiency of the practitioner. When a skilled practitioner is working at a task whose level of difficulty is appropriately engaging, he or she can slip into the sense of flow, where perception of time and space shifts and performance of the task reaches a level of ease disproportionate to its challenge.

You probably know this state as a runner. It's what keeps us involved in the sport year to year: those runs and races where everything clicks and even stretch-goal paces are manageable or, better yet, easy to achieve. Regular practice of the preceding limbs of yoga will help you reach this state: Avoid actions that cause suffering, commit to actions that increase happiness, be stable and easy in your physical pursuits, use the right breath for the moment, keep your attention on the internal experience, and practice singular focus. When you're good at these, you'll be able to find the flow state more and more often.

{ *exercise* }

Achieving *diyana* and *samadhi* (see below) is less about making them happen and more about creating the situation where they can arise. When you find yourself in the flow state, don't overthink things. Practice appreciating the moment without attachment because the more you cling to the experience, the more fleeting it becomes.

Samadhi

The goal of the practices of the first seven limbs is blissful connection, or *samadhi*. When we are in this state, we rest in our true nature, and the perceived barriers that separate us from each other and from the universal energy that permeates everything fall away. If you're lucky, you've had tastes of this bliss in your running. It can be easier to come by during periods of physical exertion like trail running, especially in picturesque natural settings with sympathetic training partners or new friends. The more we can access it in controlled settings, the more we can remember and find it again under duress in less glorious circumstances. Just as *samadhi* is the ultimate goal of yoga practice, it is also the goal of running: to be able to stay present and witness the inherent beauty in our interconnectedness, to learn the truth about who and what we are. Even with, or especially because of, the demands we put on our physical bodies, we recognize there is something more to us than the physical.

13

BREATH EXERCISES

YOUR BREATH SUPPORTS YOU not just in running but, on the most fundamental biological level, in life. Yet it is easy to go through an entire run, or a whole
day, without paying attention to your breath. Breath awareness is a shortcut to paying
attention—to noticing what is happening right now. Just as your breath has been here
your whole life and even defines your life, whatever is happening in the moment has
been here, too. You just might not have noticed. By sharpening your awareness of
your breath—the way it moves in the space of your body, its timing, and your ability
to control it—you'll be better able to pay attention to what is happening around you.
As a runner, being keenly aware of your breathing increases not only your efficiency
and endurance during a run or race but also helps you focus when things get tough,
in running and in life.

You can pay attention to the breath anywhere, anytime. Once you learn to focus
on your breathing, you need never be bored again! Sitting in traffic, waiting in line,
ticking off yet another mile in your long run, staying in a yoga pose while the teacher
adjusts other students: All of these become opportunities for breath awareness. As you
gain this awareness, you can begin to use the appropriate breath for a given activity
or pose. Appropriate breathing increases your efficiency, endurance, and focus because
it uses just the energy you need and no more, freeing you to send excess energy else-
where. The right breath for waiting in the store is not the same as the right breath for
holding plank pose or sprinting to the finish line. Follow the techniques described in
this chapter, and you'll get to know what kind of breath best supports your efforts,
moment to moment.

The Breath in Space

ON THE MAT

To begin building awareness of your breath, take a comfortable position: Sit on the mat, on a sofa, or in a chair; lie flat on the floor in corpse pose; recline onto a bolster for supported fish pose; or rest in child's pose. Breathe through your nose, or through your nose and mouth if your nose is stuffy. Observe how the breath moves in the space of your body. When you inhale, where do you feel motion? Can you exaggerate the motion? How does that feel? Can you retain awareness of it even when you return to an unexaggerated breath? What about the exhalation: Where do you feel it?

Change position. If you were lying down, take child's pose; if you were sitting, try supported fish. What changes about the places the breath moves? Where do you feel it now?

ON THE RUN

The breath that supports optimal efficient form when you run is not the same breath you have when you're reclining in bed, fully relaxed. Instead, you'll need to retain some engagement of the deep abdominal muscles to keep a steady relationship between your pelvis and your spine. This engagement will of necessity limit the amount of shape change you feel in your belly, and it will bring the action of the breath into the chest more.

Notice where you feel the breath move as you run, with special attention to how that shifts according to your pace. When you are going harder, what happens? Does the breath move higher in your chest, or lower? Can you feel more shape change when you breathe at faster paces and harder efforts, or does the breath feel more constricted then, with less motion?

Get to know what's happening with your breath when you are running well across your various paces, and you'll be able to return to the proper baseline breath when things aren't going well. Usually, you'll find that you're holding tension that impedes the free flow of the breath; remove it, and you'll be able to hold the pace with less perceived effort.

The Breath in Time

ON THE MAT

A classic yoga breath exercise is to impose a ratio on the breath, inhaling and exhaling for set amounts of time and sometimes prescribing a length to the pauses between in-

Restrictions on the Breath

The more you're aware of your breath's normal movement during your running, the more quickly you can respond if you find something amiss. If you suffer from seasonal allergies, be attuned to the allergens that can irritate your respiratory passages. Similarly, pay attention to air-quality indexes and ozone levels; poor air quality can have a big effect on your breath.

✦ *One of my coaching clients, a former NCAA Division 1-A runner and elite age group triathlete, developed exercise-induced asthma in her early forties. She had been complaining for a month or two about "dead legs" and an inability to hit her usual paces with the same perceived exertion, so we had dialed back her training and emphasized recovery. Only after an out-of-town friend visited for a training weekend and commented on her wheezing did we pick up on the signs of asthma. After her diagnosis and with medication, she's been able to get her perceived exertion and breathing back in line. If your breath has changed patterns lately, or you feel a disconnect between your breath and your pace, talk with your health care provider about what's going on.*

halation and exhalation. Here are a few simple ways to build toward this ratio breathing; do them from a comfortable seated or reclining position.

First, watch how the breath is moving across time. How long do your inhalations take? How long do your exhalations take? Are they even? Once you see how they are moving, you can begin to change them. Start by bringing the inhalation and exhalation into evenness so that they last for the same amount of time. Doing so helps balance your sympathetic ("fight or flight") and parasympathetic ("tend and befriend") nervous systems. You can breathe to a count of 4, 6, 8, or 10. The number is not important; the evenness is.

Next, notice the moment at the top of each inhalation, when you are full of breath but haven't yet begun to exhale. Draw that moment out, so that it lasts a little longer. You could pause for one or two beats, yielding a ratio of 6 to 1 to 6 to 1, inhalation, pause, exhalation, pause. (That 6 could be an 8, or the 1 could be a 2; again, the numbers are not as important as the balance between them.)

Finally, you can pull the exhalation a little longer to further engage your parasympathetic nervous system. Try adding a few beats to the length of time it takes to breathe out, bringing it to 8 or so, creating a ratio of 6 to 1 to 8 to 1. It may take you a few rounds to get the pacing right—and that may shed light on your innate tendency toward starting too fast or too slow.

After a few rounds of ratio breathing, release any imposition on the breath and let it come and go freely, observing how you feel.

ON THE RUN

You'll have natural ratios when you run, too. You might already know what they are, or you might find yourself surprised that you haven't noticed them yet. Either way, take the next few runs to observe your breath at various paces. I can't prescribe the right ratio of footsteps to breath for you; you'll have to discern that individually. But the more intimately you know your regular breath-to-step ratios, the more easily you'll be able to bring things back under control if they go off the rails. Chapter 16 describes ways to track your breath across your various paces.

Special Breath Techniques

The special breath techniques described in this section help you refine the mechanism of your breath, focusing on the muscles that aid in inhalation and exhalation. When you are in touch with these muscles, you'll be better able to find the right breath for running or any other situation. You may encounter these exercises in a yoga class or play with them at the beginning or end of your home practice. The *ujjayi* breath and the *bandhas* are appropriate for practice in the poses, as well.

UJJAYI

Ujjayi, or the warrior's breath, involves a constriction at the back of the throat to narrow the passageway of the epiglottis. By creating a narrower space, you'll challenge the muscles of respiration, especially the diaphragm, intercostal muscles between the ribs, and deep abdominal muscles (transversus abdominis and the obliques), to work in service to the breath. *Ujjayi* then becomes a form of resistance training for the breath.

To practice *ujjayi*, tighten the area at the top of your throat. You can learn to engage here by clearing your throat and bringing your awareness to that area. Hold a little muscular engagement here and breathe in and out through your nose. You'll notice a sound emanating from your throat as you breathe. Some think it sounds like Darth Vader; others think it sounds like the ocean. The sound should be loud enough that you can hear it, but not so loud that you drown out the sounds around you.

You can practice *ujjayi* breath on its own, in the ratios outlined above, or during your practice of yoga poses. As a warming breath that engages your sympathetic nervous system, it will be the right breath for flowing sequences, core work, and balancing poses; it will not be appropriate for more relaxing poses like corpse pose or those you'll find in restorative yoga (see Chapter 18). Constantly ask yourself whether the breath is serving the pose or activity.

KAPHALABHATI

One of the more challenging and energizing breath exercises in yoga, *kaphalabhati* involves forceful exhalations and then release of the muscles of exhalation. By pumping the exhalations vigorously and releasing, you'll invite the breath to enter on its own, and inhalation will take care of itself. It can be hard and messy to learn on its own, so you might like to have an instructor (and a box of tissues) nearby.

In essence, you'll pull your abdomen in and lift your diaphragm up forcefully, exhaling sharply through your nose and hearing the air puff out at your nostrils. Then relax your abdominal muscles and let the inhalation enter. If this is tough to do, pant quickly like an overheated dog, then close your mouth while keeping the sharp engagement of your belly during exhalation. Repeat at a relatively quick pace for a round of 20 exhalations or so and then take a long, full, deep inhalation before releasing the breath and breathing naturally.

NADI SHODHANA

Alternate-nostril breathing encourages single-pointed focus on the movement of the breath. In the yoga view, it works to balance the energy in the *nadis*, energy channels similar to the meridians of traditional Chinese medicine. Regardless of whether you notice this subtle action, you'll benefit from focusing all your concentration on what happens when you breathe through one nostril at a time.

To practice alternate-nostril breathing, take your dominant hand to your face. Rest the ring finger on one nostril and the thumb on the other (Fig. 13.1). Close your left nostril and breathe in through the right nostril, then open the left, close the right, and breathe out through the left. Staying here, breathe in through the left nostril, and then open the right, close the left, and breathe out through the right. Continue for a few rounds and then release your hand to your lap and notice how you feel. Are you more relaxed and balanced?

13.1 Nadi shodhana

LION'S BREATH

Lion's breath is one of the few times in yoga practice in which we consciously exhale through the mouth. (Generally, we use nasal breathing in yoga. If you find yourself breathing through your mouth during your practice of yoga poses, you may be working too hard.) This exhalation through the mouth allows us to focus on full exhalations, using them to release tension in the muscles of breathing, as well as the shoulders, head, and face.

This breath can get a little goofy. To enjoy it, take a full breath in, then stick out your tongue, exhale, and roar. Make a good loud hissing noise, "Hehhhhhhhhh," as you let the breath go, and with it, release accumulated tension. If you want to really get into lion's breath, focus your eyes on the tip of your nose as you breathe out (Fig. 13.2). Release everything you can with your loud exhalations.

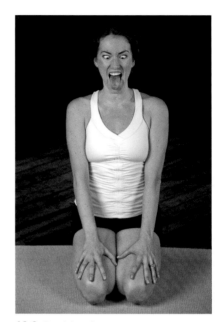

13.2 *Lion's breath*

BANDHAS

Harnessing the energetic movement of the breath, the *bandhas* are energy "locks" that engage the muscles at the pelvic floor (*mula bandha*), the diaphragm (*uddiyana bandha*), and the throat (*jalandhara bandha*) to seal in the energy of the breath. They are used in breath exercises and in class in various ways. If you find yourself in an Ashtanga class, for example, they will be cued throughout the physical practice; other classes might include reference to *mula bandha* in standing poses or during breath work. An experienced teacher can talk you through safe ways to engage the *bandhas* and prescribe exercises for home practice. (Practicing incorrectly can make you lightheaded.) For your running, knowledge of *mula bandha* can help provide a stable base for the pelvis; see Chapter 5 for more.

The Right Breath for Running

You don't need to do *ujjayi* breath or alternate-nostril breathing while you run. You don't even need to breathe through your nose exclusively, though it should be do-able at your recovery pace. Instead, you need to use the breath that provides you with enough oxygen to feed your effort. Once you've found that, you need to dial back the effort you spend on your breath so that it's as efficient as possible. This will be a process of trial and error; you'll have to figure it out both in your training and, in races, on the fly. But take heart: You have the tools to find the right breath. You've been doing it your whole life.

14

MEDITATION EXERCISES

MEDITATION TEACHES US both single-pointed focus and the ability to maintain calm awareness of many things at once while remaining detached. Meditation moves us away from the mental chatter of the ego that permeates much of our day and allows us to see that there is more to us than our thoughts. Through meditation we enter the state of *yoga* as defined in the *Yoga Sutras*: the cessation of the fluctuations of the mind.

To be able to stop the fluctuations, we must first admit how distracting they are. You probably spend much of your day in engagement with the internal chatter, the voice that pushes you to look up race times on Athlinks instead of doing your work, the self-criticism that says you're not good enough to consider working toward a particular goal time, the banal chatter about whether someone likes you, or how your job or house or car or PR or ability to put your foot behind your head defines you.

By taking time apart to meditate, you start to realize there is more to you than your thoughts. In your consciousness is a witness who watches these thoughts run through your mind. When we are able to access this witness awareness, we can maintain equanimity, balance of emotions, and an appropriate distance from the mental chatter. We are less swift to react, more measured in our dealings with ourselves and others.

While running itself can be meditative, it's useful to develop a separate sitting meditation practice. Taking even just a few minutes each day to turn your attention away from the world and toward your inner experience can have profound effects on your running and your daily life. When you run, you're forced to engage with the world, if only just to stay upright; when you sit for meditation, you are able to focus only on the experience.

The meditative method you use is less important than your consistent practice of it, and the amount of time you spend in meditation is less important than meditating regularly. Make a commitment to spend 5, 10, or 20 minutes a day in meditation for a full month, and at the end of the month evaluate how you did. Remember that results might not be quantifiable, but you'll be able to get a qualitative impression of your state of mind and centeredness during your month of practice. It will likely be all the encouragement you need to continue.

How to Sit

For these exercises, find a comfortable way to sit. You should be firmly planted in your posture, but you should feel freedom in the hips and spine. If your seat is uncomfortable, you'll spend time enduring pain in your back and hips, not freeing your awareness to concentrate. As a runner, you're probably already good at stoic endurance; you need comfort so you can experience the mental and spiritual side of meditation.

ON A CHAIR OR SOFA

If you have tight runner's hips, consider sitting in a chair or sofa. Choose one that is tall enough to let your knees rest lower than your hips (elementary school chairs are out), but not so tall that you can't rest your feet firmly on the floor (Fig. 14.1). Find a neutral position of the pelvis, aligning it so that your spine can lift up through its natural curves with no discomfort. If you're on a sofa, you can add a pillow to support the inward curve of your lower back between the couch back and your waistline.

Rest your hands so that your shoulders are relaxed: on the arms of the chair, if it has them, or in your lap, where you can place your hands palms up or down or have the palm of one hand support the back of the other. Where your hands are is secondary; finding a placement that allows you to relax is primary.

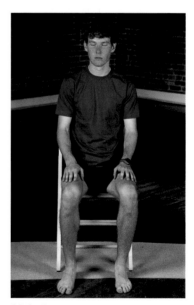

14.1 *Sitting on a chair*

ON THE FLOOR

For a more classic meditation seat, arrange yourself on the floor. Props are essential here. Lay something soft on the ground: a partially folded blanket, or a meditation rug or wide cushion. Onto that, set a prop, which can be another stack of blankets or a bolster or round cushion. Rest your sitting bones on this top prop and your shins and knees on the lower padding. Taking your sitting bones to the short end of the bolster or the corner of the stack of blankets will clear the cushioning out of the way of your knees, so that they can fall to the padding. Alternatively, you can use a yoga block, perhaps wrapped in a towel, for a firmer seat.

You can kneel (Fig. 14.2) or sit cross-legged, drawing your knees wide and removing the cross of your ankles, lining your heels up toward the midline. This position is called *sukhasana*, or easy seat (Fig. 14.3). If that doesn't work, sitting "criss-cross applesauce" with the knees supported on blankets is a good alternative (Fig. 14.4).

As you gain flexibility in the legs and mobility in the hip socket, you might enjoy sitting in *siddhasana*, or adept's pose (Fig. 14.5). For this shape, you'll cross your ankles, tucking the toes of the top foot behind the ankle of the bottom leg. *Swastikasana* (which we can call "quarter lotus") is another seat that can work; for this, build on adept's pose by pulling your top foot farther toward the bottom knee, keeping the foot tucked between the thigh and calf of the bottom leg (Fig. 14.6). If your skeletal

14.2 *Kneeling*

14.3 Sukhasana

structure allows, in time you can sit in half or full lotus pose. But you may be one of the many people for whom the extreme external rotation of the hip that lotus requires isn't feasible. Don't worry; you can still be an expert meditator sitting cross-legged or in a chair.

14.4 *Sitting with knees supported*

14.5 Siddhasana

Sitting with a Timer

Use your sports watch, an application on your smart phone, or a kitchen timer to keep track of your session. Without this accountability, you'll be tempted to jump out of your seat when things get tough. Set the timer just out of reach and then direct your gaze to the floor or close your eyes.

14.6 Swastikasana

Counting Meditation

Counting makes a good focus for your first approach to meditation. There are all kinds of patterns you can use. A simple one is to count your breaths, starting with the number 1 and building to 10, 20, or 50. You can inhale to count odd numbers and exhale to count even numbers, or inhale and exhale for one count and then move to the next number with the next breath. Choose one pattern to use for a few sessions; don't go changing the count because the one you pick is hard. When you find your attention has wandered—and it will, over and over again—go back to 1 and start over.

When you get proficient at counting up, try counting down. Start at 30, 50, or 100, and if you should get to 1, just repeat to yourself, "1, 1, 1."

Mantra Meditation

The repetition of numbers becomes a mantra, or a mind-focusing tool. You can also meditate on a specific mantra such as a word or phrase: *in, out*; *Om*; *peace* or its Sanskrit term, *shanti*; or any other syllable or string of syllables that works for you. The word you choose, while it may be powerful, is less important than the repetition of it. When you find your thoughts moving off of your mantra and onto other topics, bring them back to your mantra. You may need to do this over and over again; that's the work of meditation.

In mantra meditation—and counting is just a form of mantra—you may reach a state where you aren't actively engaged in counting, but neither are you drifting into thought. Don't be alarmed; you've moved from *dharana*, the state of intense concentration, into *diyana*, awareness of many things and nothing. If you should catch yourself in this state, you might yank yourself back out, then become upset, realizing you had "made it" as a meditator but snapped out. Don't let it faze you: Return to the single-pointed focus on your mantra and then allow the meditative bliss to seep in without forcing it. The more you practice, the more easily this will come, and you may find it feeding into your experiences in running, as well. The runner's high is one example of being in this meditative flow state. The more you practice being fully absorbed in what is happening, the more often you will find it during your running.

Moving Meditation

Once you have experience with sitting meditation, you can complement your sitting practice by employing the tools as you move. Mantra and breath awareness lend themselves well to running; see Chapter 16 for specific ways to include them in your training sessions and races.

You can also incorporate meditative techniques in your yoga practice on the mat. For example, repeat your mantra inwardly or out loud as you move through poses or hold them. Count your breaths as you hold challenging plank poses or in deep hip stretches. The more practice you gain with meditative exercises and states, the more accessible they will be across a range of situations.

I recently taught a segment of a yoga *mala*, a practice of 108 sun salutations to celebrate the summer solstice. The 108 were divided into four segments of 27 rounds each, and I led the second. The second round is dedicated to family, friends, and what we euphemistically call "precious jewels," individuals with whom we experience conflict that can teach us valuable lessons.

This reminded me of the beautiful practice of *metta,* or "lovingkindness," meditation. For each round, the yogis would choose one person, be they loved, neutral, or problematic, and keep them in mind and heart through the round.

Thus, we stood with hands to heart and thought of someone. Inhaling, we lifted them up, and exhaling, we brought them down to the mat. We lifted halfway to remember to keep our hearts open, then moved toward downward-facing dog, table pose, or child's pose (various good choices for modifications). As we rested there, we wished for this person:

May you be happy.
May you be healthy.
May you be whole.

Finally, we came to the front of the mat, folded down to seal this wish, elevated this person to the heavens, and then set them in our hearts before moving on to the next person. It was a profoundly moving experience, all the more because we kept moving along, person to person, instead of staying for too long with our emotions regarding any one individual.

By breaking down your run—the 26 miles of the marathon, for example—into dedication or appreciation for 26 different people in your life, you can make the run a celebration of your appreciation and devotion to these people. These dedications can give you strength when things get tough. Practicing sending lovingkindness to everyone, no matter how you feel about them, is sure to increase your capacity for compassion.

You can also use the motion of running as a count of its own. Count your steps to 10 over and over or count down from 50. (When I hit the straightaway during track intervals, I count down my breaths from 20. If I don't reach the finish by 1, I stick with 1, 1, 1, 1—about all I can focus on at that point.) Or use a mantra, syncing it with the sound of your footfalls and breath.

Finding a Meditation Class

Having a group for meditation can be extremely powerful, especially as you first establish the habit of meditating and when you need a boost of motivation. It's pretty easy to find a group in most cities and many towns. These could be affiliated with Buddhist or Zen centers, with yoga studios or holistic medical practices, or with major hospitals.

Classes may be run in sessions, by drop in, or both. Expect a brief lecture on an element of the practice (a "dharma talk"), a period of quiet meditation, and time to discuss the experience after.

As you get deeper into the practice, you might commit to a weekend or weeklong retreat, which take place at retreat centers, yoga ashrams, or resorts. Going on retreat allows you to deepen your practice away from the distractions and demands of your daily routine. You'll return home with a new commitment to your meditation practice.

Some centers offer running- or hiking-specific meditation retreats. Check the web sites of the Kripalu Center for Yoga and Health in Massachusetts (kripalu.org) and the Shambhala Mountain Center in Colorado (shambhalamountain.org).

PART V

PUTTING
it
TOGETHER

15

ROUTINES FOR DYNAMIC WARM-UP
BEFORE A RUN

THE STATIC STRETCHING provided by holding a yoga pose is useful, but it should not be done just before a workout. Recent studies have shown that such static stretching can diminish short-term strength in the muscles. Instead of following the old-school model of running a few laps of the track, then flinging a leg up on the fence as you fold over to stretch your hamstrings, use a dynamic warm-up. Yoga is perfect for this.

In a dynamic warm-up routine, you'll move in and out of poses without lingering in them. The goal is to move through your range of motion, priming the muscles for the work you will soon do. The dynamic warm-up helps get the appropriate muscles firing. For example, paying special attention to warming up your hip muscles, especially the glutes, ensures you are beginning your run with appropriate muscular engagement, which can help prevent injury down the line by keeping the workload in the right muscles.

Before you begin any of these routines, stand in mountain pose for a few breaths. Set an intention for your training session, so that you enter it with a clear sense of purpose. You can use this time to commit to a mantra, set parameters for your interval pacing, or simply appreciate the blessing of being strong enough to run today. Move through the dynamic warm-up with a focus on your breath. This helps set the tone for a fantastic run.

SUN SALUTATIONS WITH LUNGES

WHY: Sun salutations engage your whole body, and they use your mind and breath to synchronize your motion to your inhalations and exhalations. As such, they make a fantastic pre-run warm-up.

Standing in mountain pose,

inhale and lift your arms overhead.

Exhaling, dive forward from the hips

and come into a forward fold. >>>

exhaling, lower your body halfway to the ground, elbows in tight.

Inhaling, swing hips forward and open your chest for upward-facing dog;

exhaling, come to downward-facing dog. >>>

Inhaling, lift your back until it is parallel with the ground;

exhaling, fold again.

Inhaling, step your right foot back to a lunge; exhaling, lower your hips in the lunge.

Inhaling, step left foot back to plank,

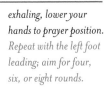

Inhaling, step right foot forward; exhaling, lower both hips to lunge.

Inhaling, step your left foot forward and lengthen your back;

exhaling, fold forward.

Inhaling, sweep your arms overhead as you rise to standing;

exhaling, lower your hands to prayer position.
Repeat with the left foot leading; aim for four, six, or eight rounds.

VARIATIONS: If you are familiar with "classical" sun salutations A and B as taught in Ashtanga Yoga and power yoga classes, with jump-backs and jump-forwards, you can remove the step to lunge and jump right to *chaturanga* and the halfway lift in sun salutations A. Do not remain in downward-facing dog for more than a breath at a time, lest you relax your hamstrings too much before your run.

Start in mountain.   Inhale to upward salute;   exhale to forward fold. >>>

Inhale to upward-facing dog;   exhale to downward-facing dog.   Inhale and jump to the
                                                                          halfway lift; >>>

Inhale to a halfway lift;

exhale and jump back to **chaturanga.**

exhale and fold.

Inhale to the upward salute;

exhale and return to mountain pose.
Repeat for three to ten rounds.

Sun salutations B include chair and warrior I; simply move with your breath.

Start in mountain.

Inhaling, come to chair pose;

exhaling, fold forward.

Inhaling, lift halfway; >>>

exhaling, push up to downward-facing dog.

Inhaling, step your right foot forward and spin your left heel down for warrior I;

exhaling, go to **chaturanga**. >>>

exhaling, take **chaturanga**.

Inhaling, go to upward-facing dog;

exhale and push up into downward-facing dog. >>>

exhaling, jump to **chaturanga.**

Inhaling, move forward into upward-facing dog;

Inhale into upward-facing dog;

exhale while pushing up to downward-facing dog.

Inhaling, step your left foot forward and spin your right heel down for warrior I;

Inhaling, jump to the halfway lift;

exhaling, fold.

Inhaling, rise to chair;

exhaling, straighten up to mountain pose. Repeat for three to five rounds.

MODIFIED SUN SALUTATIONS

WHY: There are times when you may not feel comfortable doing a full round of sun salutations. If the ground is wet, slippery, muddy, or covered in gravel, you won't enjoy bearing weight in your hands or lowering all the way to your belly. You can modify the series by skipping plank, *chaturanga*, upward-facing dog, and downward-facing dog.

From mountain pose,   *inhale and lift your arms;*   *exhale and dive forward.*   *Inhale, lift up halfway;*
     >>>

and, exhaling, take lunge in the other direction with the knee bent and the ball of the foot on the ground.   *Then, inhale to step forward into half forward fold*   *and exhale to fold completely.*
                                                >>>

exhale, fold.

Inhale, step your right foot back to lunge; exhale, lower your hips and bend your left knee more.

Inhale, push into the left foot, swivel to the right,

Inhale to rise,

exhale to reset. *Repeat and make your way back to mountain pose.*

ARROW LUNGE SEQUENCE

WHY: If you have had trouble with hip strength in the past, then the arrow lunge routine is perfect. It warms up your entire body, with a special focus on the lower legs and hips. You'll activate your glutes and the muscles that support your ankles, while waking up your sense of balance and focus. It's also a good routine if you begin your run on a gravelly road or mucky trail and don't want to put your hands on the ground.

Start in mountain pose.

Inhaling, lift your right foot, bending your right knee to 90 degrees and sweeping your arms up.

Exhaling, step your right foot back and bend your left knee into a lunge as you keep your torso on the diagonal.

Inhaling, push into your left foot and take your torso perpendicular to the ground.

>>>

VARIATION: You can build this routine sequentially, so that you start by simply lifting your leg, then replacing it. Next, step back to arrow lunge, then forward to the lifted leg, then to mountain. On the next round, include the push to bring your torso perpendicular to the floor. Continue until you've completed a few rounds of the full sequence, changing sides after each round.

Exhaling, lower your left hand and sweep your right arm to the left, taking a side stretch for the right side and deepening the stretch in the right hip flexors.

Inhale, sweeping both arms overhead;

exhale, bringing your torso back to diagonal.

Inhale and drive your right knee forward; exhale and step it down. Repeat on the other side. Three to ten rounds will warm you up.

Quick-Fix Warm-ups

If you have only a few moments before your run begins (say, while you wait for your GPS signal to lock in), try one of these quick routines to get your hips and hamstrings going.

WARRIOR III

WHY: Coming into and out of warrior III and hand-to-foot activates your glutes and hamstrings, priming you for your run. You'll also need to use your lower leg and your core for stability, locking in to focus before your workout begins.

HOW: From mountain pose, hinge forward to warrior III. Hold a long line, head to right toes. Inhale and touch your right foot down; exhale and repeat the hinge to warrior III. After 5 to 10 breaths, change sides.

Stand tall in mountain pose.

With your weight in your left leg, exhale and lift your right leg behind you as you hinge your pelvis forward to warrior III.

VARIATIONS: Your hands can be at your hips, or you can stretch your arms into a *T*. For even more challenge, extend arms overhead.

WARRIOR III AND LEG EXTENSIONS

WHY: Combining warrior III with leg extensions engages your hip flexors, which work to lift your leg forward even as you hold your core steady.

Stand tall in mountain pose.

Inhale and lift your right leg in front of you;

exhale and swing it behind you.

Inhaling, lift it in front of you again; exhale and return to mountain.

Repeat on one side for a few rounds, or alternate side to side.

VARIATIONS: Use your arms as you like to help with balance. The arms can stay overhead, swing with your torso, or bend at the elbows and then pull back as you rise to the leg extension.

Your raised leg can be bent at the knee as you lift it in front of you, or for more challenge, try to extend your knee as you lift your foot.

16

ROUTINES FOR PRACTICE
DURING A RUN

DOING YOGA during a run doesn't mean hurdling obstacles in hurdler's stretch or stopping to lunge midrun. As we've seen, there's much more to yoga than the physical poses. While the strength, flexibility, and balance you gain from the physical practice are deployed as you run, you can also use the lessons of focus and presence you've learned on the mat out on the trail.

Try using the techniques outlined below during an easy run. Once mastered, they will aid you during harder runs and whenever your mind starts to wander. Being able to come back to good form and presence of mind will improve your running immeasurably. These mental skills will allow you to bear down when you need to. You may realize you've been using these techniques already without considering them "yoga."

MOUNTAIN POSE ALIGNMENT

WHY: The more often you can muster mountain pose (Fig. 16.1), the better you'll be able to keep your form together and remain efficient. When you're feeling distracted or bored during a run, come back to mountain pose alignment. When you're feeling exhausted and miserable, come back to mountain pose alignment. Wherever you are on the spectrum of pacing and managing intensity, mountain pose alignment will help.

HOW: Before you run, take a few breaths in a steady mountain pose. Then, throughout your run, revisit the alignment principles of mountain: feet under knees under hips. Pelvis neutral. Chest broad, shoulders descending. Chin down and back. Relax everywhere you can, given the demands of what is happening right now. Once you know how to hold your core column erect and balanced, whether standing or in plank position, you can keep coming back to mountain pose during your workout.

16.1 *Mountain pose*

CONSCIOUS BREATHING

WHY: Knowing your breath's normal habits allows you to notice when there are problems and to take steps to correct them. How does your breath coordinate with your footstrike at an easy pace? At a tempo pace? At a mile pace? At a 400-meter pace? How many steps do you take as you inhale? How many as you exhale? Which foot is striking the ground when you begin your breath in? Which foot is striking as you begin your breath out?

You might find yourself surprised that you don't know the answers. They are easy enough to garner, though.

HOW: On your next few outings, pay attention to how the breath relates to your stride, answering for yourself some of the questions above. Then, in times when you find yourself feeling flustered or a little "off," compare your current breath to your breath during successful runs. Perhaps you'll find the key to restoring your sense of ease.

VARIATION: If you develop a side stitch, notice which foot is striking the ground as inhalation and exhalation begin and then change your breathing so that the other foot is hitting the ground. This alteration in breath pattern changes the position of your diaphragm relative to your abdominal organs and can reduce "cecal slap," which may be causing the stitch. And if the stitch is actually a cramp in your diaphragm, conscious attention to your breath helps relax the muscle.

MANTRAS

WHY: The Sanskrit word *mantra* translates literally as "instrument of thought." Repetition of a mantra helps harness and concentrate your thinking brain, and it can help route you into the flow state—the runner's high. Sometimes the words of a mantra are meaningful; sometimes they are not. The meaning of the words is less important than the repetition of them.

HOW: If you've drawn strength from music while running, especially music you are remembering instead of listening to passively, you've got some experience with mantra. When you put the headphones away and repeat a line or two of a song to yourself over and over, you're sharpening your experience with mantra. Don't curse yourself next time a song is "stuck" in your head on a run. Instead, loop it in your head. See if you can use a line or two from the song to help carry you into a focused, relaxed state.

Build a library of mantras to use. Some will apply for long, slow runs; others will work better for short, hard efforts. What they are isn't nearly as important as finding ones that work for you and then using them repeatedly in training. The repetition creates an association between your mind and body as you work, and it allows you to use the mantra to strongest effect during a peak run.

My favorite mantras include "form and breath," "strong and smooth," and "tall and loose." You probably have used similar ones. Even as your library of useful mantras grows, be open to receiving mantras from outside sources. A coach's comment or a spectator's sign can offer you a phrase or a word that helps you focus and push when you need to. Receive the help.

DRISHTI

WHY: The *drishti,* or gazing point, is an anchor for your awareness. In the context of an asana practice, *drishti* helps you direct your focus to a particular point—the floor in an arm balance, the core in downward-facing dog, the wall in standing balance poses. Similarly, using *drishti* on the run helps you fasten your attention to one thing. Sharpening your mental focus in this way lets you bring all your awareness to the task at hand, instead of being derailed by outside distractions.

HOW: You've probably been using this technique already, when you tell yourself to run hard to a light post, mile marker, or finish line. Setting your gaze on that object links you to it, creating an energetic lasso that helps you move forward. This can be especially helpful during track workouts, in part because they are intense and in part because the footing isn't tricky. Learning to steady your gaze on one object, even as your body is moving through space, is an example of the process of *dharana,* or single-pointed concentration.

On a trail run, the trail itself becomes the object of your *drishti,* a moving focal point. In order to avoid falling, we by necessity must become aware of each root, rock, and rivulet on the path and then pass over them. This echoes the process of *diyana,* or meditative awareness. We notice objects that lie in our path, and instead of stopping to investigate them in detail or evaluate them, we pass over them.

Minimalist Shoes

The trend in running shoes is toward "barefoot" models that offer little support for the feet. This is wonderful if it fosters lower-leg strength and supports balance in the body. It's easy, however, to get swept up in the latest trend and overdo the amount of barefoot or lightly shod running you do. Be conservative in your use of lightweight shoes, so that your body has time to adapt to the mileage, and use yoga to support lower-leg health.

✦ *When it comes to shoes, use the guideline of sending energy only where you need it. A minimal shoe may be just the thing for you, allowing the most efficient movement path. Or it may create undue tension in other parts of your body. Remember: Your goal is balance; make choices that align with that goal.*

17

ROUTINES FOLLOWING
AN EASY RUN

WHEN YOUR RUN has been easy, or even moderate, a more vigorous yoga practice can follow, building strength, flexibility, and focus. If you can move right into the practice from your run, you'll enjoy the benefit of warm and relatively loose muscles. If you need to slot it a little later in the day, include some warm-up poses, like those in Chapter 15, before moving into the main segment of the practice.

Depending on your needs and where you are in your training cycle, the post-run routine can be challenging or relaxing. Even close to competition, it's good to maintain your core strength and work on balance; just be sure you aren't overdoing it. Your state of recovery from day to day will show you whether you're working too hard on the mat, but your breath will show you from moment to moment.

There are a nearly infinite number of post-run practices you can create for yourself, using the poses described in Part II of this book. Below you will find a few examples. In general, you can slot in a few standing poses or balance poses and then some core work on the floor, followed by hip stretches. Depending on your own needs and imbalances, you may choose more standing work or more floor work, more strengthening or more stretching. Let these routines inspire you to follow the cues from your body and breath.

STANDING BALANCE POSES

WHY: Practicing standing balance poses taxes your hips and legs to stabilize you. You'll build strength in your standing-leg hip and lower leg while receiving a stretch for the raised or back-placed leg. Once you've held each pose for 5 to 10 breaths, move to the next, and after doing all three, change sides.

HOW: In dancer, you'll be on the right leg with the left knee bent; for more, lean forward from the pelvis. Next, cross your left ankle over your right knee for standing pigeon; for more, bend your right knee and squat. Finally, step your left foot forward for pyramid, folding into it until you feel a pleasant stretch. Repeat on the second side.

Move from dancer   *to standing pigeon*   *to pyramid.*

HAND-TO-FOOT SEQUENCE

WHY: Another approach to standing balance poses, this hand-to-foot (or hand-to-strap-to-foot) sequence also builds hip and lower-leg strength in the standing leg and flexibility in the raised leg, additionally stretching the inner thigh of the raised leg and strengthening the hip flexors. Hold each of these for at least 5 breaths, and build up to 10 breaths each.

HOW: For hand-to-foot, stand on the right leg and hold your left leg in front of you. Next, swivel your left leg to the left for an inner-thigh stretch. Returning the leg in front of you, hold it unbound in a leg lift as your hands rest on your hips. Finally, swing your raised leg behind you as you hold your back and pelvis parallel to the floor in warrior III.

VARIATIONS: For more ease, go through the sequence with your raised leg bent, and skip warrior III or keep your back-leg toes on the ground. Or use a strap to aid the connection of your hand and your foot.

Move from hand-to-foot   *to hand-to-foot side stretch*   *to leg lift*   *to warrior III.*

STANDING HIP STRETCHES

WHY: A series of standing poses will stretch your legs, hips, back, chest, and arms simultaneously, while engaging leg and core strength. Move through the sequence on one side and then the other. Start with 5 breaths in each; build to 10 or more.

HOW: For warrior I, step your left leg forward, bend your left knee 90 degrees, drop your right heel, and lift your arms to a comfortable position. Next, open to warrior II by orienting your pelvis and shoulders to the right and lowering your arms parallel to the floor. Drop your left elbow to your left knee and take your right arm diagonally overhead for side angle, and then straighten your left knee and lift your right arm overhead for triangle.

VARIATIONS: Try the sequence in reverse, noticing how it affects your body and breath. Or pulse in and out of the poses, bending and straightening the forward leg in warrior I and warrior II and from side angle to triangle and back.

Move from warrior I   *to warrior II*   *to side angle*   *to triangle.*

PLANK SERIES

WHY: Taking plank pose in different orientations to gravity strengthens the muscles that support your hips, shoulders, and everything in between.

VARIATIONS: Once you can hold each pose for 10 breaths, you can add another round of each.

Lifting and lowering a leg increases the intensity of plank and reverse plank. In side plank, you can lift and lower the top leg, or lower the bottom hip toward the ground, then lift it again.

Taking plank and side plank on your forearms rather than your palms alleviates strain on your elbows and wrists while challenging the muscles that stabilize your shoulder.

Hold plank,   *side plank,*   *and reverse table or a full reverse plank for 5 to 10 breaths each.*

Variation: side plank with leg lifted   *Variation: reverse table*

DYNAMIC CORE SEQUENCE

WHY: Roll-ups and roll-downs require control over the articulation of the spine, working the smaller muscles that help control its flexion and extension.

VARIATIONS: Bend the knees to lighten the work of the sequence; straighten your legs during roll-downs, roll-ups, and leg lifts to intensify.

Move from a seated position   *through a roll-down*   *into a leg lift,*

then roll up and repeat.

After five or more rounds, remain on your back and drop the knees from side to side in oblique twists for 10 breaths or more.

Finish with a lift and lower into bridge articulations for 5 to 10 breaths.

BOAT SERIES

WHY: Boat poses strengthen the muscles that stabilize the core and pelvis, with special attention to the hip flexors.

Hold one to five rounds of boat pose and then rest.

Follow with a twist from boat pose for 5 to 10 breaths,

resting again before lowering from boat to half boat and lifting back up 5 to 10 times.

IT BAND SERIES

WHY: This sequence of poses targets the IT band, releasing tension along the connective tissue and muscle of the outer hip and thigh.

With your right leg on top, move from cow-face pose

into half Lord of the Fishes.

Then recline in half Lord of the Fishes

and segue into a cross-legged twist by taking your knees close and dropping them to the left. Hold each pose for 10 to 20 breaths before moving to the next and then repeat on the other side.

PIGEON FLOW

WHY: Pigeon pose targets the musculature of the outer hip, particularly the glutes and piriformis. The forward fold stretches the outer hip and back, while the backbend addresses the front of the chest and the front of the back-leg hip.

Start with 5 to 10 breaths in lizard lunge,

then walk your front leg into pigeon pose and fold forward for 10 to 20 breaths.

Finish with 5 to 10 breaths in the pigeon backbend.

HEAD-TO-KNEE FLOW

WHY: Head-to-knee allows you to target the hamstrings and inner thigh muscles of one leg at a time while also stretching the back.

Move from head-to-knee

to revolved head-to-knee

to Lord of the Fishes, enjoying 10 or more breaths in each and moving through the sequence on one side before repeating on the other.

LUNGE SERIES

WHY: Holding lunge poses stretches the hip flexors and hamstrings of opposite legs while releasing tension in the inner and outer hip.

HOW: Stay in each pose for 5 to 15 breaths, moving to the next pose in the series before repeating on the second side.

Hold low lunge,

optionally including the quadriceps stretch.

Segue into lizard lunge

and runner's lunge.

ROUTINES FOLLOWING
A HARD RUN OR RACE

YOGA AFTER a difficult workout or race is beneficial because even if you're at the end of your season and won't be running for a few days or weeks, you need to stay limber for life.

Finish-Line Stretches

When you finish a long or hard race, deep stretching is not in order. But combined with some light running or a walking cool-down, a few well-timed poses can stave off the lockdown in your muscles. Here are some to slot in between trips to the water and food tables and awards ceremony.

STANDING CAT-COW

WHY: Moving your spine through flexion and extension helps release tension that accumulates in your back during a race. As a bonus, the standing version doesn't require you to get down on the ground.

HOW: From standing, bend your knees slightly and rest your hands on your thighs. As you inhale, lift your tailbone, broaden your chest, and look forward (Fig. 18.1). As you exhale, scoop your tailbone under, round your upper back, and drop your chin to your chest (Fig. 18.2). Continue back and forth for a few rounds.

VARIATION: You might like to slide your hips a little side to side or drop one shoulder and then the other forward to release more muscles in your back.

18.1 *Standing cow*   **18.2** *Standing cat*

SQUAT

WHY: Squatting relieves tension in your back and gently stretches your thighs, hamstrings, and calves.

HOW: Squat down, allowing your heels to lift off the ground if they need to.

VARIATIONS: You can choose a tight or a wide squat, with your legs together or apart.
     For a deeper stretch for your back, hold on to a table leg or a friend's hands and lean away from the support (Fig. 18.3).

To add a twist, take your left hand to your left knee and your right hand to the ground. Push into your left hand and look over your left shoulder (Fig. 18.4). Hold for a few breaths, then repeat on the other side.

18.3 *Squat with a partner*

18.4 *Twisting squat*

DOWNWARD-FACING DOG WITH A PROP

WHY: This gentler version of downward-facing dog doesn't invert your head far below your heart (a bad idea shortly after a major physical effort). But you'll get all the benefits of the stretch of your hamstrings, as well as a shoulder stretch.

HOW: Find a chair, picnic table, or car hood to use as a support. Take your hands to it, then walk your feet back as you hinge at the hips to form an L shape (Fig. 18.5).

18.5 *Downward-facing dog with a chair*

VARIATIONS: Bend your knees to customize the stretch for your hamstrings. Or bend one knee and shift your hips to the other side to stretch your IT band and outer hip. Then repeat on the other side.

For a partner version of the stretch, hold a friend's forearms as you both lean away from each other into the *L* shape (Fig. 18.6).

18.6 *Downward-facing dog with a partner*

NECK AND SHOULDER STRETCH

WHY: Your trapezius muscles can get surprisingly tight during a race. This stretch helps release the tops of your shoulders and your neck.

HOW: Lay your right forearm across your lower back and hold both hands at the left side of your waist. Drop your left ear toward your left shoulder until you feel a release on the right side, and hold for a few breaths (Fig. 18.7). Repeat on the other side.

VARIATION: Angle your face up or down to find a different stretch along the right side of your neck.

18.7 *Neck and shoulder stretch*

Inverted Stretches

After a key workout or a low-priority, short race, light stretching can help you unwind and speed your recovery. A mellow version of the routines outlined in Chapter 17 could work, provided you pay close attention to the sensation in your body and stay far away from any intensity.

A routine of inverted stretches at the wall is an effective way to help your muscles relax while receiving the benefits of inversion, including the draining effect of edematous fluids that accumulate in your lower legs during a tough run. For the sequence, you'll need a wall, a closed and locked door, or a coffee table or ottoman.

After moving through the asymmetrical stretches on the left leg described below (hamstring stretches, half happy baby, and figure 4), repeat on the right. Then move into the symmetrical stretches to finish. In each of the poses, stay for 10 breaths or longer.

LEGS UP THE WALL

WHY: Inverting with your legs up the wall (Fig. 18.8) drains swelling in your legs, settles your pelvis and back into relaxation, and offers a gentle stretch for your chest.

HOW: Sit with one hip very close to the wall. Swing your legs up as you recline on your back. You may need to scoot closer to the wall—or farther away from it, if your hamstrings are tight. Your arms can rest at your hips in an inverted *V*, at the sides in a *T*, bent at the elbows in a *W*, in a *V* overhead, or overhead with hands touching, like the *A* in the "YMCA" dance.

VARIATION: If your back aches or you don't have a wall handy, you can do the pose with your calves on a chair (Fig. 18.9) or a coffee table. This reduces the hamstring stretch, but it makes a fantastic choice for relaxing your back.

18.8 *Legs up the wall*

18.9 *Legs to a chair*

COBBLER

WHY: Cobbler (Fig. 18.10) stretches the inner thighs of both legs simultaneously.

HOW: Bend your knees and point them toward 3 o'clock and 9 o'clock as the soles of the feet meet and the pinky toes touch the wall.

VARIATION: If your knees roll in toward the center or the stretch is too intense, prop up your knees with your hands.

18.10 *Cobbler at the wall*

HAMSTRING STRETCHES: CENTER, OUTER, INNER

WHY: Paying attention to all the muscles that comprise your hamstrings group allows you to see where your flexibility is most specifically limited. It also allows you to apply just the right degree of intensity, given the workout you've just completed.

HOW: From your legs up the wall position, move your left heel off the wall as you find a stretch for the center of your left hamstrings (Fig. 18.11).

Stretch your outer left hamstrings by moving your left leg to the right. Keep the back of your pelvis level on the ground, and you'll find the stretch when your foot is somewhere across the midline of your body, but probably no farther than the right side of your body (Fig. 18.12). Stay in the pose for 5 to 10 breaths or more.

Look for an inner hamstring stretch by moving your left heel to the left, no farther than a few inches to the left of your body. You might need to slide your foot higher into the space above your shoulder to feel the stretch (Fig. 18.13). Stay in the pose for 5 to 10 breaths or more.

VARIATIONS: In each of these stretches, you can hold the back of your leg, or use a strap to catch the ball of your left foot. For less stretch, bend your knee more; for more stretch, straighten the knee.

18.11 *Center hamstring stretch*

18.12 *Outer hamstring stretch*

18.13 *Inner hamstring stretch*

HALF HAPPY BABY

WHY: Half happy baby at the wall (Fig. 18.14) gives a gentle stretch to your inner thigh muscles.

HOW: From your inner hamstring stretch at the wall, bend your left knee and drop it toward your left armpit, aligning your left shin parallel to the wall and your left foot parallel to the floor.

VARIATIONS: Hold anywhere on the left leg, from the back of the left knee to the left foot.

For more stretch, straighten your left knee, taking your foot off to the side of your shoulder.

18.14 *Half happy baby*

FIGURE 4

WHY: Figure 4 gives a stretch similar to pigeon pose, but this orientation (Fig. 18.15) can alleviate the pressure on the knee.

HOW: Take your left ankle across your right thigh, rolling your left knee in the direction of the wall.

VARIATIONS: If you want more stretch, bend your right knee and place the sole of the right foot on the wall. For still more, slide your right foot down until you feel a pleasant stretch in the outer left hip.

18.15 *Figure 4*

STRADDLE

WHY: The inverted straddle (Fig. 18.16) offers a different approach to stretching the inner thighs.

HOW: Take your feet wide, heels to the wall.

VARIATION: To lessen the intensity, put your elbows on the floor and hold your thighs in your hands, propping up your legs from below.

18.16 *Straddle at the wall*

BRIDGE

WHY: Doing bridge at the wall (Fig. 18.17) stretches the front of the hips—an area that is closed off as you rest in legs up the wall—and offers a relatively easy approach to shoulder stand.

HOW: Take the soles of the feet to the wall and push into them, lifting your hips. Walk your shoulder blades toward each other and support your lower back with your hands, elbows propped on the floor.

VARIATION: If this is tough on your neck, add a folded blanket under your shoulders so your neck curve doesn't flatten.

18.17 *Bridge at the wall*

SHOULDER STAND

WHY: Shoulder stand (Fig. 18.18) calms your nervous system while gently working your core.

HOW: From bridge at the wall, stretch one leg and then the other up toward the ceiling. Keep your hands behind your lower back for support.

VARIATIONS: As in bridge at the wall, putting a blanket under your shoulders while keeping your head lower, on the mat, can ease any strain on your neck.

You can keep your feet reaching for the ceiling or try a few alternatives: plow pose, in which your feet stretch past your head; cobbler pose, with your feet touching over your groin; straddle; or a slow bicycle action to stretch the hip flexors and quads. Move slowly and intentionally.

18.18 *Shoulder stand*

TWISTS

WHY: Twisting at the wall (Fig. 18.19) stretches your hips, works your spine, and broadens your chest and shoulder muscles. In addition, the support of the wall beneath your feet is a useful prop for twisting.

HOW: From legs up the wall, bend your knees and walk your feet to the right, so that your outer right foot is on the floor and the soles of your feet are stacked on the wall. Open your left arm to the left.

VARIATIONS: Depending on your preference, you can stay very tight toward the wall, or slide your hips away from it to change the experience.

Try taking your right hand to your left knee or keep it spread to the right.

Repeat on the other side.

18.19 *Twist at the wall*

LEGS UP THE WALL OR CORPSE

WHY: Finish in legs up the wall or flat in corpse (Fig. 18.20) to begin integrating the work of your mellow session. Stay for five minutes or as long as time allows.

HOW: For a deluxe version of legs up the wall, add padding under your pelvis to elevate it. Set it six inches away from the wall, so that your tailbone can sink into the space between the support and the wall. You can also cover yourself in a blanket, or add an eye pillow to your eyes or forehead (Fig. 18.21).

VARIATION: If you prefer, lie flat in corpse pose instead.

18.20 *Corpse*　　　　　　　　　　　　**18.21** *Legs up the wall*

Restorative Yoga

After a very hard run or race, your muscles don't need more work. They need rest. It's not the time for strength-building poses or even for much stretching, as vigorous stretching can compound the inflammation in your soft tissues. Instead, a gentle restorative sequence of light stretching and relaxation is in order. The effects of this practice are subtle but profound. While you shouldn't feel any intensity in any of the poses, there are deep shifts that happen on an energetic level. Resting in these supported poses engages your parasympathetic nervous system, inviting your body to relax, restore, and recover.

You need not do these poses immediately after a hard workout or a race. Later in the day, when you are clean, dry, and fed, is a fine time. A few props will come in handy: a yoga bolster or a few pillows from the sofa or bed, a stack of blankets, an eye pillow, and a wall or a closed, locked door.

Each of these poses should feel supremely comfortable. Arrange yourself so that you feel completely supported, and use your eye pillow whenever you can. Stay in each for at least 5 and up to 15 minutes.

SQUAT

WHY: Squatting releases tension in your back and legs; squatting on a bolster (Fig. 18.22) lightens the strain on your knees and removes the balance challenge.

HOW: Sit on a bolster with your legs in a squat.

18.22 *Squat on a bolster*

FISH

WHY: A well-supported backbend stretches your chest muscles while requiring no effort.

HOW: Line up the bolster to run the length of your spine, then lie back over it. Support your head and neck with a blanket if you like. Spread your arms out to either side (Fig. 18.23). Use blocks to elevate the bolster if you like.

18.23 *Supported backbend*

PRONE TWIST

WHY: Twisting with your belly to the bolster (Fig. 18.24) gives a gentle hip, back, and chest stretch and provides a strong sense of support.

HOW: Sit with the short end of a bolster or the narrower end of a folded blanket next to your hip. Turn to frame the bolster with your arms and then lower your belly and chest to it. Your knees can spread and your head can rest wherever it feels most comfortable.

18.24 *Prone twist with a bolster*

SIDE BEND

WHY: The supported side bend (Fig. 18.25) addresses the side of the ribcage and waist, a frequently neglected area. Openness here equates to better breathing.

HOW: Sit a few inches from the long side of the bolster or a folded blanket. Lie on your side over it, with the bottom end supporting your lowermost ribs. Use a pillow between your lower arm and head, and rest your hands together overhead.

18.25 *Supported side bend*

CHILD'S POSE

WHY: Resting in child's pose on the bolster (Fig. 18.26) releases tension in your back, thighs, and ankles without placing too much stress on your knees and feet.

HOW: Kneel with your knees on either side of the bolster or a stack of blankets and then lay your belly on the support. Rest on your forehead, or turn from one cheek to the other after a few minutes.

18.26 *Child's pose with a bolster*

LEGS UP THE WALL

WHY: The supported version of legs up the wall (Fig. 18.27) confers all the benefits listed above, with the bonus of a gentle backbend.

HOW: Lay your bolster or a folded blanket with its long edge six to eight inches from the wall. Rest the back of your pelvis on this support as you prop your legs up the wall. Let your tailbone sink into the space between the cushion and the wall. Take your arms off to your sides.

18.27 *Supported legs up the wall*

RECOMMENDED RESOURCES

Books

YOGA FOR ATHLETES

Capouya, John. *Real Men Do Yoga: Twenty-One Star Athletes Reveal Their Secrets for Strength, Flexibility, and Peak Performance.* Deerfield Beach, Fla.: HCI, 2003.

> This entertaining book intersperses testimonials from pro athletes with descriptions of basic poses.

Couch, Jean. *The Runner's Yoga Book.* Rev. ed. Berkeley, Calif.: Rodmell, 1990.

> Couch's classic book outlines a specific set of Iyengar-based postures that benefit runners.

Douillard, John. *Body, Mind, and Sport: The Mind-Body Guide to Lifelong Health, Fitness, and Your Personal Best.* New York: Three Rivers, 2001.

> Douillard, an Ayurvedic specialist, details nasal breathing practices and yoga routines to incorporate into your training.

Rountree, Sage. *The Athlete's Guide to Recovery: Rest, Relax, and Restore for Peak Performance.* Boulder, Colo.: VeloPress, 2011.

> Chapters on restorative yoga and meditation help athletes balance their work with yogic rest.

————. *The Athlete's Guide to Yoga: An Integrated Approach to Strength, Flexibility, and Focus.* Boulder, Colo.: VeloPress, 2008.

An explanation of how yoga and training should fit in inverse proportion, with an overview of yoga, the asanas, and sample training plans that include yoga.

————. *The Athlete's Pocket Guide to Yoga: 50 Routines for Flexibility, Balance, and Focus.* Boulder, Colo.: VeloPress, 2009.

A spiral-bound pictorial practice guide with routines for every point in the training cycle.

YOGA HISTORY, PHILOSOPHY, AND SANSKRIT

Feuerstein, Georg. *The Yoga Sutra of Patañjali: A New Translation and Commentary.* Rochester, Vt.: Inner Traditions, 1989.

Detailed explication of the *Yoga Sutras.*

Lowitz, Leza, and Reema Datta. *Sacred Sanskrit Words for Yoga, Chant, and Meditation.* Berkeley, Calif.: Stone Bridge, 2005.

Definitions of more than 160 Sanskrit terms shed light on yoga philosophy and history.

Mitchell, Stephen. *The Bhagavad Gita: A New Translation.* Pittsburgh: Three Rivers Press, 2002.

The *Bhagavad Gita* in a modern translation with a wonderful, clear introduction.

Singleton, Mark. *Yoga Body: The Origins of Modern Posture Practice.* New York: Oxford University Press, 2010.

An investigation into the roots of the modern practice of yoga.

YOGA PRACTICE

Baptiste, Baron. *Journey into Power: How to Sculpt Your Ideal Body, Free Your True Self, and Transform Your Life with Yoga.* New York: Fireside, 2003.

A catalog of power yoga for personal transformation that takes a holistic approach to mindful living and to diet.

Faulds, Richard. *Kripalu Yoga: A Guide to Practice On and Off the Mat.* New York: Bantam Dell, 2006.

A complete introduction to the Kripalu approach.

Iyengar, B. K. S. *Light on Yoga*. New York: Schocken Books, 1994.

> The book that has influenced generations of Western yogis.

Kaminoff, Leslie, and Amy Matthews. *Yoga Anatomy, 2nd ed*. Champaign, Ill.: Human Kinetics, 2011.

> Beyond its clear insight into the anatomy of the asanas, this wonderful book connects embryology and breathing to the poses, and roots yoga philosophy in the physical structures of the human body.

Lasater, Judith. *Relax and Renew: Restful Yoga for Stressful Times*. Berkeley, Calif.: Rodmell, 2011.

> Description of the practice, psychological, and physiological mechanisms of restorative yoga.

Lee, Cyndi. *Yoga Body, Buddha Mind*. New York: Riverhead, 2004.

> Investigation of the intersections between yoga and Buddhism, with detailed explanations of the asanas and instructions for personal exploration.

Schiffmann, Erich. *Yoga: The Spirit and Practice of Moving into Stillness*. New York: Pocket Books, 1996.

> This fabulous resource offers an accessible approach to meditation, as well as clear descriptions of the poses.

MEDITATION

Brach, Tara. *Radical Acceptance: Embracing Your Life with the Heart of a Buddha*. New York: Bantam, 2004.

Kornfeld, Jack. *A Path with Heart: A Guide Through the Perils and Promises of Spiritual Life*. New York: Bantam, 1993.

Nhat Hanh, Thich. *The Miracle of Mindfulness: An Introduction to the Practice of Meditation*. Boston: Beacon, 1999.

Salzberg, Sharon. *Lovingkindness: The Revolutionary Art of Happiness*. Boston: Shambhala, 2004.

DVDs

YOGA FOR ATHLETES

Benagh, Barbara. *Yoga Complete for Athletes* (2005).

Blue Dog Yoga. *Power Yoga for Endurance Athletes* (2005).

Dubs, Karen. *Flexible Warrior: Yoga for Triathletes* (2006–2011).

Rountree, Sage. *The Athlete's Guide to Yoga: A Personalized Practice* (2008).

Tarpinian, Steve, and Mary Angela Buffo. *Yoga for Endurance Athletes* (2006).

Yee, Rodney. *Yoga Conditioning for Athletes* (2000).

ACTIVE/POWER

Kest, Bryan. *Power Yoga* (2004).

Rea, Shiva. *Yoga Shakti* (2004).

YIN/MEDITATION

Grilley, Paul. *Yin Yoga* (2005).

Powers, Sarah. *Insight Yoga* (2005).

Online Resources

CLASSES

yogavibes.com

> At YogaVibes, you can stream real classes with the country's best teachers and their students. Visit my "Yoga for Athletes" channel there for dozens of practices for runners, including specific classes for core strength, hip flexibility, and recovery.

FINDING A TEACHER

yogajournal.com

> Yoga Journal's web site provides content from the magazine; home practice routines; a Sanskrit glossary; a pose finder; and a directory of yoga teachers, studios, and retreats from around the world.

yogaalliance.org

> The Yoga Alliance is a registry of teachers with at least 200 hours of training. The site offers a directory of registered yoga teachers, both in the United States and abroad. Visit these sites for directories of teachers specializing in individual styles:

anusara.com

ashtanga.com

bksiyengar.com

kripalu.org

kundaliniyoga.com

yinyoga.com

FINDING A RETREAT

eomega.org

> The Omega Institute offers workshops in upstate New York, throughout the country, and abroad.

esalen.com

> Esalen, in Big Sur, California, presents more than 400 workshops a year.

kripalu.org

> The Kripalu Center for Yoga and Health hosts a wide range of programs in western Massachusetts.

shambhalamountain.org

> The Shambhala Mountain Center offers an annual retreat on meditation for runners.

GEAR

gaiam.com

> Gaiam offers yoga props—including latex-free mats, jute yoga rugs, and cork accessories—as well as clothing, DVDs, books, and a variety of natural living products.

huggermugger.com

> Hugger Mugger sells a wide range of props, including bolsters in various shapes, sizes, and fabrics.

prana.com

> Look to prAna for eco-friendly mat options and fair-trade-certified clothing, worn by the models in this book.

SUBJECT INDEX

Abdominal muscles, 51, 81, 97, 140
Ability, testing, 115
Aerobic base, building, 113
Ahimsa, 130
Alignment, 16, 117, 120
Allergies, 141
Anusara
    described, 120
    using, 118 (table)
Aparigraha, 130
Asana, 4, 23, 67, 119
    described, 133–134
Ashtanga
    described, 120
    Primary Series of, 120
    using, 118 (table)
Asteya, 130
Asthma, 141
Athlete's Guide to Recovery, The (Rountree),
    5, 116
*Athlete's Guide to Yoga: A Personalized
    Practice* (Rountree), 125
Awareness, 15, 135, 140
    breath, 19, 134, 139, 151
    mind-body, 9, 11, 126

Back, strong, 61, 81, 120
Back extension, 61, 97
Backbends, 10, 13, 36, 115
    active/passive, 84
Balance, 3, 4, 5, 17, 81, 93, 141, 171
    arm, 110, 136
    body/space, 10–11
    building, 6, 7, 10, 19
    core and, 97
    finding, 6–7, 110
    front-to-back, 94, 97
    injuries and, 105
    left-to-right, 100
    maintaining, 9, 10
    mind, 11
    shoes and, 174
    spirit, 11
    top-to-bottom, 102
    work-rest, 11
Baptiste Power Yoga, 119
Barkan
    described, 121
    using, 118 (table)
Barkan, Jimmy, 121
Base period, 113, 114, 119, 120, 121, 122

Bhagavad Gita, 129
Bikram
    described, 121
    using, 118 (table)
Body
    listening to, 135
    mind and, 9
Brahmacharya, 130, 131
Breath, 135, 136
    awareness of, 19, 134, 139, 151
    counting, 141, 151, 152
    exercises, 15, 18, 115, 129, 140–141
    footfalls and, 142, 152
    imposition of, 141
    pace and, 140, 142
    restrictions on, 141
    running and, 140, 145
    in space, 140
    techniques, 142–144
    in time, 140–142
    warrior's, 142
    yoga and, 140–141
Breathing, 9, 15, 52, 105, 139
    adjusting, 17
    alternate-nostril, 145
    conscious, 172–173
    correct, 134
    focus on, 81
    form and, 16, 17
    inhibiting, 17
    perceived, 141
    rhythmic, 17
    toxins and, 18
Build period, 121, 122
Burnout, 10

Calisthenics, 133
Center of gravity, 11
Centeredness, 148
Cheating, 131
Chest muscles, 97
Chest openness, 120

Choudhury, Bikram, 121
Cleanliness, 126, 131
Confidence, gaining, 131
Connections, 11, 135
Consciousness, 147
Consistency, importance of, 113
Contentment, 31, 132
Cooling down, 185
Core
    balance and, 97
    breath for, 142
    building, 4, 58, 122
    maintaining, 12, 122
    stable, 51–52
Core exercises, back-extension, 84
Core fusion yoga
    described, 122
    using, 118 (table)
Core yoga, using, 118 (table)
Counting meditation, described, 151
Coveting, 131
Csíkszentmihályi, Mihály, 136

Deconditioning, 73
Desikachar, T. K.V., 129
Devi, Nischala Joy, 129
Dharana, 135–136, 151
Dharma talk, 153
Diaphragm, 51, 142
Diyana, 151
    described, 136–137
Drishti, 136
Dynamic movement, 6, 10

Efficiency, 4, 16, 17, 73, 131, 174
    breathing and, 139
    maintaining, 134
Elbows, building, 110
Emotions, 147, 152
Endurance, 100, 131, 148
    breathing and, 139
    keys to, 16–18

Energy, 19, 131, 133
    breathing and, 139
    conserving, 17
    freeing up, 132
    universal, 137
Envy, 130, 131
Equanimity, developing, 132
Erector spinae muscles, 51
Exercise, 135
    meditative, 151–152
Exhalation, 18, 23, 81, 140, 141, 142, 151,
    152

Firmness, softness and, 52
Fitness, 18, 113
Flexibility, 36, 61, 123, 171
    building, 5, 6, 23, 31, 175
    hip, 12, 133
    leg, 3
    stability and, 100
    stiffness and, 9
    strength and, 4, 7, 23, 93, 100, 129
Flow yoga, 117, 122, 137
    breath for, 142
    described, 119
    using, 118 (table)
Fluidity, stiffness and, 4
Focus, 16, 18, 81, 114, 117, 134, 136, 142,
    147, 171
    breathing and, 139
    building, 133, 175
    running and, 15
    tools for, 151
Footfalls, 17
    breath and, 142, 152
Form
    breathing and, 16, 17
    efficient, 16, 17
Forrest, Ana, 119
Forrest Yoga, 119
Forward motion, emphasizing, 6
Free flow, 6

Gannon, Sharon, 119
Goals, 19, 61, 131, 132, 137, 147
    race, 133
    training, 123, 124
    workouts and, 18
Gym-strength routines, 6
Gymnastics, 133

Hamstrings, 10, 94, 97, 124
    stretching, 93, 113, 157
Happiness, 131, 132
Hatha, 120
    described, 119
    using, 118 (table)
Heart of Yoga, The (Desikachar), 129
Hip flexors, 10, 94, 95
    building, 58
    suppleness of, 93
Hips, 52, 148
    building, 4, 102
    stability of, 23
Home practice, 124–126, 142
Honesty, practicing, 130
Hot yoga, 123
    using, 118 (table)
Hurdler's stretch, 171
Hypermobility, 6

Iliotibial (IT) band, 9, 51
Imbalance, 93, 100
    injuries and, 9, 10, 105
Incontinence, 71
Inhalation, 23, 81, 140–141, 142, 151, 152
Injuries, 117, 124
    balance and, 105
    imbalance and, 9, 10, 105
    inefficient running and, 4
    mental, 10
    overuse, 9, 93, 105, 130
    preventing, 5, 52, 122, 157
    training and, 130
Intensity, 114, 115, 135, 188, 194

Interconnectedness, 137
Intercostal muscles, 142
Internal dialogue, 131
Internal experience, focus on, 134
Ishvara pranidhana, 131, 133
Isometric exercises, 5, 23
Isotonic exercises, 5, 23
Iyengar
   described, 120
   using, 118 (table)
Iyengar, B. K. S., 120, 129

Jealousy, 130
Jivamukti Yoga, 119
Jois, K. Pattabhi, 120

Karma yoga, 129
Kinetic chain, 97, 100
Knee trouble, 5
Kripalu
   described, 121
   using, 118 (table)
Kripalu Center for Yoga and Health, 121,
   153

Lateral movement, 100
Leary, Timothy, 135
Life, David, 119
Light on Yoga (Iyengar), 120
Locks, 51, 71, 120
Lovingkindness, 152
Lower body, upper body and, 81
Lower leg
   running stride and, 73
   strengthening, 174

Mala, 152
Mandala, 6
Mantras, 133, 136, 151, 152, 15
Meditation, 113, 129, 132–133, 147, 153
   counting, 151
   incorporating, 152
   mantra, 151

mental/spiritual side of, 148
   moving, 151–152
   sitting and, 151–152
Mental skills, 13, 113, 171
Metta, 152
Mind-body awareness, 9, 11, 126
Mind-body-breath component, 122
Mindfulness, practicing, 115
Mobility, 4, 6, 23, 67
   stability and, 52
Mood, 115
Motion, fluidity of, 4
Mula bandha, 51
Muscular engagement, 115, 157
Mysore, described, 120

Negative behaviors, avoiding, 130–131
Neural connections, 10
Niebuhr, Reinhold, 115
Niyama, described, 131–133
Numbers, repetition of, 151

Obliques, 142
   external/internal, 51
Off-season period, 114, 120, 123
1–2 (or 1/2), described, 119
1–3, described, 119
Openness, strength and, 81
Overreaching, 130
Overstretching, 97, 123
Overthinking, 137

Pace, 16, 131, 141
   breath and, 140, 142
   recovery, 145
Pain
   avoiding, 73
   back, 5, 94
Parasympathetic nervous system, 141, 194
Pelvic floor, maintaining, 71
Pelvis, 10, 16, 17, 51, 94, 97
   spine and, 52
   stable, 81

Performance, 130, 136
Periodization, principles of, 122
Perspective, conferring, 18–19
Pilates
    described, 122
    using, 118 (table)
Poses, 3, 4, 61, 117, 134, 135, 139
    arm-balancing, 136
    balance, 105, 124, 133, 142
    challenging, 16, 124
    dynamic, 52
    easy, 13
    holding, 157
    kneeling, 76
    relaxing, 121
    restorative, 18
    squatting, 73
    standing, 6
    static, 52
    strength, 23, 194
Post-run routine, challenging/relaxing,
        175
Power yoga
    described, 119
    using, 118 (table)
Prana Flow Yoga, 119
Pranayama, described, 134
Pratyahara, described, 134–135
Precious jewels, 152
Props, using, 124, 125
Psoas, 51, 52
Psychological tools, work/rest balance
        and, 114–116

Quadratus lumborum, 51
Quadriceps, 93, 94

Range of motion, 4–5, 6, 88, 157
Rea, Shiva, 119
Recovery, 5, 12, 121, 145, 188, 194
    importance of, 116
Rectus abdominis, 51
Relaxation, 17, 18, 131, 134, 188, 194

Resilience, 23, 51
Rest, 124, 194
    importance of, 116
    recovery and, 12
    work and, 5, 11, 93, 113, 114
Restorative yoga, 114, 116, 194–195
    described, 121
    using, 118 (table)
Roach, Geshe Michael, 129
Rotator cuffs, strain on, 124
Running, 16–17
    breath and, 145
    focus and, 15
    inefficient, 4
    medium-intensity, 12
    yoga and, 12, 15, 142, 171

Sagittal plane, 100
Samadhi, described, 137
Santosha, 131, 132
Satchidananda, Swami, 129
Satya, 130
Saucha, 126, 131, 132
Season, yoga practice and, 11–12, 132
Self-control, 131
Self-criticism, 19
Self-improvement, 18
Self-knowledge, 18, 133
Self-study, 131
Shambhala Mountain Center, 153
Shanti, 151
Shin splints, 76
Shoes, 73
    balance and, 174
    motion-control, 102
    stabilizing, 123
Shoulders, building, 110
Side bends, 10
Sitting
    comfortable way for, 148–150
    meditation and, 151–152
Snapping back, 15–16
Softness, firmness and, 52

Space, 136
  breath in, 140
Spine, 51, 148
  long, 81
  pelvis and, 52
  strong, 133
Split stance, 31
Squatting, kneeling and, 79
Stability, 4, 23, 67, 102, 123
  flexibility and, 100
  mobility and, 52
Sthira, 4, 23, 52
  sukha and, 5, 93, 129
Stiffness, 5
  flexibility and, 9
  fluidity and, 4
Strength, 51, 122, 131, 133, 171
  back, 98
  building, 4, 5–6, 19, 31, 52, 58, 61, 120,
    131, 175
  flexibility and, 4, 7, 23, 93, 100, 129
  hip, 3
  maintaining, 119, 121
  mental, 4
  openness and, 81
  tapping into, 114–115
Strength training, 5
Stress, 114, 116
  adapting to, 5
  training, 123
Stretches, 3, 7, 73, 84, 121, 123
  asymmetrical, 188
  deep, 185
  finish-line, 185
  hamstring, 96
  hip, 175
  hurdler's, 171
  intensity of, 36
  inverted, 188
  light, 188, 194
  lower back, 94
  proper, 6
  static, 157

strap, 82, 96
symmetrical, 188
Stride, 4, 5
  running, 23, 31, 73, 76, 88
Sukha, 4, 23, 52
  sthira and, 5, 93, 129
Sutras, 4, 129, 130
Svadyaya, 131, 133
Sympathetic nervous system, 141

Tapas, 131, 132–133
Tension, releasing, 17, 18, 140
Thighs, 94
  strengthening, 102
Tibialis muscles, 76
Tightness, 5, 94, 97, 122
Time, 136
  breath in, 140–142
Toxins, breathing and, 18
Training, 3, 124, 129
  breaks from, 114
  complementing, 117
  cycles, 11, 119, 120, 122, 123, 175
  focusing on, 114
  injuries and, 130
  plan, 122, 129, 132
  sessions, 152, 157
  undermining, 118
Transversus abdominis, 16, 51, 142
Tuning in/tuning out, 135
2–3 (or 2/3), described, 119

Ujjayi, 145
  described, 142
Upper body
  lower body and, 81
  running stride and, 88

Variety, importance of, 113
Video classes, 125, 126
Vinyasa, 120, 122
  described, 119
  using, 118 (table)

Warm-ups, 134, 157, 175
   quick-fix, 168
   sequences of, 158–167
Warm yoga, 123
Weaknesses, 100, 122
Work/rest balance, 5, 11, 93
   psychological tools for, 114–116
   yoga and, 113–114
Workouts, 13, 132, 135
   goals and, 18
   intensity of, 122
   planning, 126
   recovery and, 121
   yoga and, 185
Wrists, building, 110

Yamas, described, 130
Yoga
   achieving, 130
   as action, 129
   defined, 4, 9, 129, 147
   restorative, 114, 116, 118 (table), 121,
      194–195
   running and, 12, 15, 142, 171
   styles of, 118, 118 (table), 123
   workouts and, 185
Yoga classes, 123–124, 126
   choosing, 118–122
"Yoga for Athletes" classes, 126
Yoga practice, 115, 123, 132, 135
   adjusting, 12, 19
   medium-intensity, 12, 116
   rigorous, 114, 122, 175
   space for, 125–126
   time for, 126
Yoga studios, 118, 125, 153
   home practice and, 126
Yoga Sutras, 4, 129, 133, 147
Yoga teachers, 124
   looking for, 122–123
Yogalates
   described, 122
   using, 118 (table)
YogaVibes, 125

POSES INDEX

Arrow lunge sequence, described, 166–
    167
Arrowhead plank
    described, 54
    photo of, 54

Bandhas, 120, 142
    described, 144
Biceps stretch
    described, 83
    photo of, 83
Bird dog
    described, 61–62
    photo of, 61, 98
Bird dog with backbend, photo of, 62
Bird dog with rounded back, photo of, 62
Boat
    described, 58, 181
    photo of, 58, 97, 181
Boat to half boat
    described, 60
    photo of, 60
Boat with a twist
    described, 59
    photo of, 59

Boat with extended arms and legs, photo
    of, 59
Boat with extended legs, photo of, 58
Bow, 99
    described, 66
    photo of, 66, 95
Bridge, 84, 98
    described, 70, 192
    photo of, 70
Bridge at the wall, photo of, 192
Bridge on a block, 99
    described, 86–87
    photo of, 87, 95
Bridge on a block with feet apart, photo
    of, 87
Bridge on a bolster, 95
    described, 86
    photo of, 86, 99
Bridge using arms, photo of, 70
Bridge with hands on floor, photo of, 70

Center hamstring stretch
    described, 190
    photo of, 190
Chair pose, photo of, 162

Chaturanga, 113, 114, 120
  described, 55
  photo of, 55, 161, 162, 163
Child's pose, 104, 113, 124, 140, 152
  described, 76, 197
  photo of, 76
Child's pose with a bolster, photo of,
  197
Child's pose with raised hands, photo of,
  76
Cobbler, described, 189
Cobbler at the wall, photo of, 189
Cobra, 84, 98
  described, 63
  photo of, 63
Conscious breathing, described, 172–173
Corpse, 134
  described, 194
  photo of, 194
Cow-face, 101
  described, 39
  photo of, 39, 181
Crane (a.k.a. Crow)
  described, 110
  photo of, 110
Cross-legged reclining twist
  described, 46
  photo of, 46

Dancer, 103, 105
  described, 109
  photo of, 109, 176
Dancer with strap, photo of, 109
Dolphin, 96
  photo of, 54
Downward-facing dog, 152
  photo of, 53, 96, 158, 160, 162, 163
Downward-facing dog with a partner,
  photo of, 187
Downward-facing dog with a prop
  described, 187
  photo of, 187
Drishti, described, 173–174

Dynamic core sequence
  described, 180
  photo of, 180

Eagle, 103, 105
  described, 107
  photo of, 107
Exalted warrior, 101
  photo of, 25

Figure 4
  described, 191
  photo of, 191
Firefly, photo of, 111
Fish, described, 195
Fish on a bolster, described, 84
Fish on blocks, 99
  described, 85
  photo of, 85
Front stretch, poses for, 99
Full reverse plank, photo of, 179

Half bow, 95
  photo of, 66
Half happy baby
  described, 191
  photo of, 49, 191
Half kneeling, half squat
  described, 80
  photo of, 80, 104
Half kneeling, half squat with shin and
  ankle stretch, photo of, 80
Half Lord of the Fishes, 101
  described, 44
  photo of, 44, 181
Halfway lift, photo of, 160, 161, 163
Hamstring strap stretches, 96
Hamstring stretch with leg extended,
  photo of, 47
Hamstring stretch with leg moved inward,
  photo of, 48
Hamstring stretch with leg moved
  outward, photo of, 48

Hamstrings
    described, 47–48
    poses for, 96
Hand-to-foot
    described, 107
    photo of, 103, 108
Hand-to-foot, head turned, photo of, 108
Hand-to-foot, holding foot, photo of, 108
Hand-to-foot, leg extended, photo of,
    108
Hand-to-foot sequence
    described, 177
    photo of, 177
Head-to-knee
    described, 42
    photo of, 42, 96, 182
Hero
    described, 78
    photo of, 78
High lunge
    described, 31
    photo of, 31

Inner hamstring stretch
    described, 190
    photo of, 190
Inner/outer hip balance, poses for, 101
Inner thigh
    described, 49
    photo of, 49
IT band series, photo of, 181

Kaphalabhati, described, 143
Kneeling, 76
    photo of, 149

Leg extensions
    described, 169–170
    photo of, 169
Leg lifts
    described, 68
    photo of, 68
Legs to a chair, photo of, 189

Legs up the wall
    described, 189, 194, 197
    photo of, 189, 194
Lion's breath
    described, 144
    photo of, 144
Lizard lunge, 95
    described, 34
    photo of, 34, 101, 182, 183
Locust
    described, 65
    photo of, 65, 66, 98
Locust with arms extended, photo of, 65,
    98
Lord of the Fishes, 101
    described, 44
    photo of, 44, 182
Low lunge, 95
    described, 32
    photo of, 32, 94, 183
Lower leg strengthening, poses for, 103
Lower leg stretching, poses for, 104
Lunges, 7, 10, 31, 36, 171
    described, 183
    photo of, 158, 159, 160, 161, 162, 163,
        164, 165, 166, 167

Modified sun salutations, described,
    164–165
Mountain, 157
    described, 172
    photo of, 100, 158, 160, 162, 163, 164,
        166, 168, 172

Nadi shodhana
    described, 143
    photo of, 143
Narrow squat
    described, 74
    photo of, 74, 104
Neck and shoulder stretch
    described, 188
    photo of, 188

Oblique twists
    described, 69
    photo of, 69
Outer hamstring stretch
    described, 190
    photo of, 190
Outer thigh and hip stretch
    described, 50
    photo of, 50

Passive backbend, photo of, 84, 99
Passive backbend with bolster
        perpendicular to spine, photo of, 85
Pigeon backbend, 99, 101
    described, 41
    photo of, 51, 182
Pigeon backbend with quadriceps stretch,
        photo of, 41
Pigeon flow
    described, 182
    photo of, 182
Pigeon forward fold
    described, 40
    photo of, 40, 101, 176
Pigeon forward fold, standing, photo of,
        40
Pigeon pose, photo of, 182
Plank, 58, 97, 134, 152
    described, 52–53
    photo of, 53, 179
Plank with opposite arm and leg lifted,
        98
    photo of, 53
Prone twist, described, 196
Prone twist with a bolster, photo of, 196
Pyramid, 101
    described, 29
    photo of, 29, 176
Pyramid with active back, photo of, 29
Pyramid with passive back, photo of, 29

Quadriceps stretch, photo of, 183

Reclining cow-face, 101
    photo of, 39
Reclining half Lord of the Fishes, 95,
        101
    described, 45
    photo of, 45
Reclining hero, 95, 99
    photo of, 78
Reclining pigeon, 101
    photo of, 40
Reclining twist with stacked knees,
        photo of, 46
Reclining twist with straight leg, photo
        of, 46
Reverse plank, 98
    described, 57
    photo of, 57, 97
Reverse table, 98
    photo of, 57, 179
Reverse table with leg lifted, photo of,
        57, 98
Revolved head-to-knee, 101
    described, 43
    photo of, 43
Rishi fold
    described, 30
    photo of, 30
Rock, 104
    described, 77
    photo of, 77
Rock with blanket, photo of, 77
Roll-down/roll-up
    described, 67
    photo of, 67
Root lock, 51
    described, 71
    photo of, 71
Runner's lunge
    described, 35
    photo of, 183
Runner's lunge with ankle stretch, photo
        of, 35, 96

Runner's lunge with calf stretch, photo of, 35

Seated forward fold, photo of, 37
Shoulder circles
    described, 82
    photo of, 82
Shoulder-pressure pose
    described, 111
    photo of, 111
Shoulder-pressure pose, ankles crossed, photo of, 111
Shoulder stand
    described, 193
    photo of, 193
Siddhasana, photo of, 150
Side angle, 101
    described, 28
    photo of, 28, 178
Side plank
    described, 55–56
    photo of, 56, 179
Side plank on forearm, photo of, 56
Side plank on knees, photo of, 56
Side plank with leg lifted, photo of, 179
Single-legged chair, photo of, 100, 102
Sitting on a chair or sofa
    described, 148
    photo of, 148
Sitting on the floor, described, 149–150
Sitting with knees supported, photo of, 150
Squat, described, 186–187, 195
Squat on a bolster, photo of, 195
Squat with partner, photo of, 187
Squat with twist
    described, 89
    photo of, 89
Squat with twist, hand on knee, photo of, 90
Squat with twist, hands clasped, photo of, 90

Standing balance poses, 136
    described, 176
    photo of, 176
    single-leg, 100, 106, 115
Standing cat
    described, 186
    photo of, 186
Standing cow
    described, 186
    photo of, 186
Standing forward fold, 96
    photo of, 36
Standing hip stretches
    described, 178
    photo of, 178
Standing pigeon, photo of, 176
Straddle, described, 192
Straddle at the wall, photo of, 192
Sukhasana, photo of, 149
Sun salutations, 6, 152
    modified, 164–165
Sun salutations with lunges
    described, 158–163
    photo of, 158, 159, 160, 161, 162, 163
Supported backbend, photo of, 195
Supported legs up the wall, described, 197
Swastikasana, photo of, 150

Table, 98, 152
Thoracic rotation, 88
Thoracic twist, photo of, 88
Threading the needle, described, 88
Threading the needle to elbow, photo of, 88
Threading the needle with leg moved outward, photo of, 89
Threading the needle with shoulder lowered, photo of, 89
Tight forward fold, described, 36–37
Toe balance
    described, 74
    photo of, 74, 103

Toe stretch
  described, 79
  photo of, 79, 104
Tree, 103, 105
  described, 106
  photo of, 106
Triangle, 101
  described, 27
  photo of, 27, 178
Triceps stretch
  described, 83
  photo of, 83
Twist at the wall, photo of, 193
Twisting lunge
  described, 33
  photo of, 33, 95
Twisting squat, photo of, 187
Twists, 10, 88
  described, 193
  reclining, 101

Upward-facing dog, 84, 120
  described, 64
  photo of, 64, 158, 160, 162, 163

Warrior I, 95, 101
  described, 24
  photo of, 24, 99, 162, 163, 178
Warrior II
  described, 25
  photo of, 25, 101, 178
Warrior III, 101
  described, 26, 168, 169–170
  photo of, 26, 103, 168, 169, 177
Wide forward fold, described, 38
Wide forward fold, shift, photo of, 38
Wide forward fold, standing straddle, 96
  photo of, 38
Wide forward fold with twist
  described, 90
  photo of, 90
Wide squat, 104
  described, 75
  photo of, 75

ABOUT THE MODELS

THOMAS GRAHAM is a senior at Cary Academy in Cary, North Carolina. For the past five years he has trained and competed in cross-country and distance track races around the country. Since starting competitive distance running, Thomas has trained without any major injuries and largely attributes that to the implementation of yoga and similar strength and flexibility training as part of his regimen. As a freshman, he was third nationally in the USATF Age Group Cross-Country Championships. As a senior, he finished ninth in the United States in the 2011 Footlocker Cross Country Championships in San Diego. He has run 14:45 for 5K and 9:00 for 2 miles. He will attend Stanford University and compete on both the cross-country and track teams.

KRISTIN WATSON was a 400-meter hurdler at West Virginia University from 1998 to 2002 and a member of the distance medley team that won the 2000 Penn Relays. In college she met her future husband, Peter, also a member of the WVU track and field team, member of the Canadian National Track and Field Team, and current men's cross-country coach at the University of Virginia. This relationship sent her on the journey to become a distance runner, and she has completed several half-marathons around the country. In addition to her work as an elementary school art teacher, she teaches group exercise and finds great satisfaction in the diversity and combination of group fitness, the practice of yoga, and daily runs.

ABOUT THE AUTHOR

SAGE ROUNTREE is an internationally recognized authority in yoga for athletes and an endurance sports coach with certifications from USA Triathlon and RRCA; she also holds a PhD in English literature. She is the author of *The Athlete's Guide to Yoga* (2008), *The Athlete's Pocket Guide to Yoga* (2009), and *The Athlete's Guide to Recovery* (2011); creator of *The Athlete's Guide to Yoga* DVD (Endurance Films, 2008); and a regular contributor to *Runner's World, Yoga Journal,* and *USA Triathlon Life.*

An Experienced Registered Yoga Teacher with the Yoga Alliance, Sage is on the faculty at the Kripalu Center for Yoga and Health and teaches at YogaVibes.com. Her students include casual athletes, dedicated age-groupers, Olympians, and many University of North Carolina athletes and coaches.

Sage competes in running races from the 400 meter to the ultramarathon and triathlons from the supersprint to the Ironman; she was a member of Team USA at the 2008 World Triathlon Championships. She lives with her husband and daughters in Chapel Hill, North Carolina, where she co-owns the Carrboro Yoga Company and directs its yoga teacher training program. Find her online at sagerountree.com.